·BEYOND·
VISUALIZATION

...

·VIKI KING·

NEW WORLD LIBRARY
San Rafael, California

Published by New World Library
58 Paul Drive
San Rafael, CA 94903

Cover design: Cassandra Chu

Text design: Cassandra Chu

Typography: TBH/Typecast

Library of Congress Cataloging-in-Publication Data

King, Viki.
    Beyond visualization : feel it in your heart, have it
in your life / Viki King.
        p.   cm.
    ISBN: 931432-83-9 (alk. paper)
    1. Self-actualization (Psychology)   2. Visualization.
I. Title.
BF637.S4K55   1992
153.3'2—dc20   91-38389
                                                  CIP

ISBN: 931432-83-9
First Printing, 1992
Printed in the U.S.A. on acid-free paper
10 9 8 7 6 5 4 3 2 1

DEDICATION

This book is dedicated to me.

Writing it helped me
to tell the truth
to myself
about what I want.
Here's a blank line:

_____

(your name here)

You can dedicate it to yourself.
What do you want?

ACKNOWLEDGMENTS

Did you ever read an acknowledgment in a book that admonished, "Nobody helped me. I did it all myself." That kind of book couldn't ever get itself published. To bring something from nothing to beingness requires help. You need to let magic happen. When you're lucky, that magic comes through people both dear and new who you can appreciate and love and have a whole bunch of fun with.

Here's some people I appreciate and love and have a whole bunch of fun with: Thanks to all at New World Library. They are a wonderful pleasure to know and work with! Imagine what a help that is. Katherine Dieter is very talented; wait until you read her novel. Marc Allen is the publisher and the kind of person you could hang out with and listen to music. He's unassuming while publishing books that will inform us into the twenty-first century. Leslie Keenan is senior editor. I always liked her and respected her and somewhere into part two of our dealings, I fell in love with her. Sue Arnold did an excellent job on copy editing. Since you have this is in your hands, the man to thank is Munro Magruder, marketing maven par excellence. He got it onto the airwaves and into the bookstores so it could fall off the shelf into your hands.

Thanks to Bridget Leonard, she plugs people together; it lights up the world. Thanks to Nina Reznick for her generous lawyering. Thanks to Barbara Elman Schiffman for her great work, as always, typing this thing. She's very good at her work and I appreciate her.

I have so very many loved ones. Here are some who put their sweet touch to this book pie:

Thanks to Paula Shtrum, excellent novelist and a good friend who is near and dear and there.

Thanks to Jeff Swartz for jacuzzi conversations and promenades to the beach.

Thanks to Leigh Charlton for her eagle eye and her midwestern heart.

And finally, a dear thank you to Buddy Collette for who he is, for what he has shared with me in wisdom and love, for . . . *everything.*

CONTENTS

"He who knows
that enough is enough
will always have enough."
Lao Tzu

"No matter where you go;
there you are."
Buckaroo Bonzai

PART ONE

Beyond Visualization

■ *What Is Beyond Visualization? And Why Would I Want to Go There?*

Feelization is the next step beyond visualization. It's the art of having your heart's desire. Now. Right now. You can come true today.

What Is Feelization?

There's something you want. What is it?

_____

(your heart's desire here)

Close your eyes. Feel how your body is feeling right now. On a scale of one to ten, how many watts are circulating in you? Now feel that you have the thing you want. How many watts does that feel like? Now feel your present wattage. Amp up or ease down to the new wattage. Feel it. Notice what it opens in your body. Is your heart pounding faster; are you clearing your throat; are you breathing deeper from your stomach? Feel how you feel when you have what you want. Feel it. You got it. That's Feelization. Pass goals; go directly to how you want your goals to make you feel *now*.

How Is Feelization Different from Visualization?

With visualization you picture what you want to have and manifest the thought into the thing outside yourself. It's great and it works. (Get Shakti Gawain's book *Creative Visualization*. She's got a real knack.)

We're so good at using visualization naturally that we do get our thoughts manifested, but that's not satisfying our hearts. Twenty years ago in Silva Mind Control classes people were happily creating parking spaces. Now they want the cars.

You could have it all, but if it doesn't feel as if you've got it, or if it doesn't feel as if it's what you wanted it for, then you keep wanting more and more and it feels like less and less. When you go directly to the feeling you want, you can have it now. In visualization, thoughts equal matter. In Feelization, feelings matter.

Einstein said, "$E = MC^2$," which means that energy can be transformed into matter. The Feelization formula is "Feelings matter, and when they do, that equals everything." So you can have the yacht—with Feelization you can feel deeply good aboard the yacht.

Why Goals Are a Crock

My friend's baby was crying. She said, "I don't know what he wants." I said, "Well, you can rule out a Jaguar." The point is this: When we are little, we are very funda-mental about our needs and wants. We need our diapers changed. We need food. We want love. When we don't get those fundamental needs and wants met, we get very sophisticated about goals (e.g., "I'll be rich and then I'll get girls" or "I'll be president of Megacorp and then I'll show them"). We work so hard on *separating* ourselves from others, when what we really want is to be connected. We want love.

Now we can go directly to what we wanted in the first place. Here's how:

Let's Play "So That . . . "

State a goal that you have right now. Keep saying *so that* until you get down and down and find out what you want the goal to really get for you.

Here's an example: Lulu wanted to be on the cover of *People* Magazine . . . *so that* her Aunt Rose would see it in the supermarket and take it home and read about her . . . *so that* Aunt Rose would call up all the ladies in the neighborhood and tell them . . . *so that* Lulu's mother would hear about it . . . *so that* Lulu's mother would call Lulu and invite her to dinner.

Here's what happened with Lulu: Once she found out why she wanted to be on the cover of *People* Magazine, she went directly to what she really wanted. She called her mom. Her mom invited her to dinner. *P.S. As a result of reuniting with her mother, Lulu got a lead in a Broadway play. Any day now she may or may not be on the cover of* People *Magazine, but it's okay with her either way.*

What Kind of a Book Is This If It Doesn't Get Me My BMW?

You may say, "Pooey, I want what I want. Why do I have to settle for dinner?" Because dinner is what you really want. All roads lead to love. What we're doing here is allowing ourselves to spend less energy *getting* there and more direct experience *being* there.

Now you might say, "Okay, I'll take the love, but I still want my BMW." The fastest way to your BMW is Feelization—have it in your heart right now. Why wait to get there? Be there. Being there is the fastest way to getting there. Have it in your heart, then have it in your driveway.

You Can Have Anything You Want; What Do You Want?

This is a trick question. We humans have been known to spend great gobs of our lives trying to come up with clear answers to this question. Here's a very simple technique . . . We'll ask. Fill in these blanks with one word each:

My name is _____ .

I want _____ .

I need _____ .

Look at your want and need for a few minutes. You can be thoughtful.

Now fill in these blanks with one word each (they can be the same words as your want and need):

If I had _____ ,

then I could have _____ .

Now switch those two answers:

If I had _____ ,

then I would have _____ .

The key to getting to the bottom of your heart is to switch your want and your need.

Here's an example from my life: "If I had the money, then I could move to the beach." I flipped them over: "If I move to the beach, then I will have the money." I moved to the beach, and guess what? The money came in my mailbox. If I didn't live there, it wouldn't be my mailbox. (It wouldn't be my money.)

Why This Simple Switch Works

We often put the cart before the horse. When we switch them around, we can move forward. For instance, we think we need the great job so we can have self-respect. Switch it. If we respect ourself, we could get the job. We have a tendency to go for the want. If we went for the need instead, the want would take care of itself and we would get much, much more than what we wanted.

How to Read This Book

This is a "do" book. You'll participate. You'll feel. You'll get new results. Here's what actions you can take today. Here's the results you'll get today. Tomorrow you can get some more. You don't have to be "on the way"; you are the way. Be happy now, no waiting.

When Do I Get Mine?

Transformation is very quiet, very small. It happens on a day you don't notice. If you were watching, you'd stop it. You'd want drama; you'd want to work hard at it and suffer. You've done enough of that. Now *let yourself have it!*

■ *Why You Don't Think That You Get What You Want*

Brace yourself. You always get what you want even if it looks like you don't.

Here's great good news: Think of where you are in your life now. Here's the deal: Where you are is where you want to be. Now you may say, "What are you, nuts? Here? Here in the buzzsaw department of Sears?"

Where you are is where you want to be. See that the life you have now, you really, truly, actually want. Once you see that you created it, you can get all happy with your powers. You can enjoy the *benefits* of what you created. And, once you see that where you are is where you want to be, you can identify and clarify ways to change where you are.

Here are four questions to ask yourself:

- Am I ready to have what I want?
- Do I think I deserve it?
- Am I afraid to have it?
- Do I want the impossible dream?

Now let's look at these four questions and the variations on each. You'll recognize yourself here. It's okay.

Am I Ready to Have It?

Here's how smart you are. You've resigned yourself to *not getting what you want until you're ready to have it.* Here's an example: You pray for a Ferrari and you don't get it. Maybe you live in a high auto theft neighborhood. When you say "I want a Ferrari," suddenly you're evicted. This is good! You need to get out of that neighborhood because it's not the right place to park a Ferrari. If you're not ready to have your life change, then you're not ready to have your dream come true yet. That's fine. You'll have your hands full getting ready. You'll get your Ferrari. First, learn to drive.

Do I Trust That I Can Get It?

Name at least three fears that occur when you aren't sure you're going to get what you want. Some examples: You talk yourself out of wanting it; you stop yourself from going after it; you live in a state of wanting something and never getting it. All kinds of drama go on around "Can I have what I want?" Of course you can have it. There. That settles that. Now go after it, and in the going after it you'll see if you really want it.

What if I Go for It and Don't Get It?

What you're going to do is feel and learn and go on. It is always a gain.

Sometimes you stay stuck in trying because you're not yet ready to *not* have it. Example: I know an aspiring actor who has Burt Reynolds's phone number and assumes that when he calls, Burt will hire him for the next movie and he'll be a big hit. He believes all he has to do is make that one phone call and his life will be answered—happily ever after. And yet he doesn't make the call.

Sometimes we keep our dream a dream until it's time to drop it or act on it. Know what you want your wants for. For this aspiring actor, the dream gave him insight into what he needed to do to get himself ready for fame. Before he made the call that was going to make him famous, he realized he wanted to take an acting class, get photos, iron his shirt.

Once you are willing to say "I want this thing," commit to it and go. You will get the best and highest good for you.

Is It Time Yet?

One of my 20-year-old students said, "I'm so tired of failing!" I said to her, "You haven't failed, you just haven't yet succeeded." There are times when you feel that you absolutely know your wish has your name on it, you just know it belongs to you and you're not getting it and you don't understand why. It's only a matter of time frame; all the unseen elements are still moving into place. You are going along on one rail and your wish is going along on another rail, and you'll meet down the line someplace. The wish *does* belong to you; it *does* have your name on it; you're just getting readier and readier to receive it.

You can use this book as part of getting ready to have what you want. There are even exercises for getting ready. You can actually identify ways in which you're not ready.

In the meantime, look at what you're getting ready for.

Listen when people who have succeeded at something talk about it. They didn't just step into the accomplishment cold; they *opened space* for it.

Someone who wins the lottery thought about it before, played it before, put energy there, bought the ticket. Your magic will come to you. Practice letting it come in.

Yeah, But . . .

This is an all-time favorite for most of us. Actually, you can recognize this more easily in somebody else. If a friend calls you up and says, "I want to be on the Broadway stage," and you say, "Great! Do it!" and then the friend will say, "Yeah, but I have to lose twenty-five pounds." You can then see the obstacle between where your friend is *now* and where he or she wants to be: "I want to be a star" is the want. "I have to lose twenty-five pounds" is the obstacle.

You are very clear about your want, and you're very clear about what's keeping you from what you want. Great. Now what's really keeping you from what you want? My theory: *You are not willing to have what you say you want for the person you are now.* In other words, you want to be somebody else. You want to be somebody who is twenty-five pounds lighter. You are not willing to have what you want until you are the person you want to be.

See how you set up a dream to require that you change something in yourself? Losing twenty-five pounds is probably a bigger challenge than being a star. Go ahead and be a star, if that is your heart's desire. The twenty-five pounds is another dream you can make come true or not as you wish.

So watch your yeah-buts. When they come up, write them down. You will identify what scares you, what you think is the highest, most insurmountable problem that you have. And when you do that, you can begin to look and see . . . must you lose twenty-five pounds? This came from someone who called me, and my feeling was that the best way for her to be on the Broadway stage was to take her twenty-five pounds with her. Without her twenty-five pounds she wouldn't be the robust, strong character that she is now.

Ask yourself, "When will I be willing to have what I want?" This will make nice and clear what stops you, what scares you, who you think you have to be other than who you are now, and who you feel you want to be. You might think, "If I am 150 pounds, I don't deserve this. If I am 125 pounds, then, ah, I can have it." Accept who you are, *as is*.

Have what you want now by accepting who you are now.

Do I Think I Deserve It?

Take a piece of paper. Divide it down the center. Start a conversation between yourself and yourself. On one side start with saying "I don't deserve it," and on the other side have yourself say, "Oh yeah, why?" And keep going back and forth and back and forth, and continue to have a conversation with yourself and find out what reasons you have for not deserving your heart's desire. I'll give you a clue. Here are three of them:

- I'm too selfish.
- I'm above it all.
- If I get it I have to share it.

Keep going until you hit paydirt, usually meaning a swell of emotion that comes out of you and is released and you feel a whole lot better and then you have an unabashed urge to run right out and buy.

Is My Dream Big Enough?

A friend of mine had an idea that she would like to be a rich and famous writer and a rich and famous actress and have a house on the beach. I think she had a couple of other things thrown in too . . . a car, thin thighs. You might say, "Well, is that dream big enough?" No. It isn't. The point is this: If your dream is just for a mere castle, just to make a million dollars, just to have all the pedigreed dogs in your backyard—that's not enough. It's not enough because all those things are outside yourself. A dream that is big enough is one that is within you. Wish for an essence, a feeling from within, a sense of peace, an appreciation of life, a willingness and an openness and an ability to experience love.

And so, when you are inventing your future, if your dream is for bigger and bigger outsideness, then what happens is your heart gets smaller and smaller on the inside, and then you need bigger and bigger dreams to fill the smaller and smaller opening in your heart. If you choose wants that open your heart, you'll find joy and satisfaction in your heart's desire. You'll have it all.

Do I Try and Still Not Get What I Want?

The activity of trying will keep you trying. It will never get you what you want. There must be a benefit in trying or you wouldn't be doing it. If you try and then don't get it, that's exactly the result you had in mind. Getting what you want, you probably believe, has a great deal of responsibility to it, and you don't want the responsibility. If you try and you don't get it, you can feel that you're still honorable.

This happens a great deal with people applying for jobs that they don't want to have. One of my clients needs other people to say, "You can't have this job. You're overqualified," so that he won't have to take the job. Eventually he won't need to go out and look for a job that he doesn't want in the first place.

Start identifying where you repeatedly try for a result that you don't get and see what benefit you get from trying. See that what you really want is just to be off the hook. If you want to be off the hook, then be off the hook and don't even bother trying.

Can I Say "I Want What I Want"?

It's okay to want what you want. This is, for some of us, a revolutionary concept! What kinds of thoughts well up from you when you say these words? What messages do you remember from your family?

Here's your assignment: Write very quickly five beliefs, phrases, comments, or bromides you heard from your family when you were a kid and asked for what you wanted. It could be the voice of your kid sister: "He always gets what he wants and I never do"; or your mother: "You can't always have what you want."

You know them; you've got them; write them down. You'll be amazed at how, once you write them, you will gasp and release yourself from their tyranny and then go get what you want.

Am I Afraid to Have It?

Do you remember all those unhappily-ever-after stories from when we were little kids? You rub the lamp, the genie comes out, you get three wishes. Fine. Was there ever a story that was happy—the characters got their three wishes and they were all wonderful? There was always a trick to it. "Be careful what you wish for; you may get it"— pooey on this concept, pooey! Be honest in your heart, and make the wishes you wish. This is where Feelization works beautifully. All you have to do is feel it, feel in your heart what you want to feel like, not what you think it would look like. Feel it, and the details will take care of themselves. When you make an honest wish, enjoy what it feels like; then you will enjoy what it looks like when it comes true.

Feel it first, then see how it comes out. If you picture it first, it may not come out that way and you may not recognize it, or it will come out exactly as you pictured it but won't feel good. Always manifest from feeling and your genie can get you exactly what you want.

P.S. If you don't like what you get after you get it, wish again—wishes are unlimited!

Am I Afraid I'll Get It and Then I Won't Want It?

Here's what to do about this one: Get it, and if you don't want it, then get something else. There's no law that says you're stuck with it. You're not obligated.

A lot of times we feel that if we want something, in some way it's going to cost us and in some way it's going to require that we're saddled with the thing forever. The way to work on this is to give yourself little things. Wish for possible things that you can get within the next five minutes. Get it and see how that feels. If you don't like it, then get something else . . . and get something else. And you'll begin to start seeing what you're willing to accept and live with after you've gotten it, and what you're not willing to have.

I painted my bedroom. I woke up one morning and looked up at the ceiling and there were big splotchy spaces where I had not painted my bedroom, so I called somebody. I had my bedroom painted again. Here's the upshot: I don't even look at the ceiling when I wake up; I look out to sea. But if it was a splotchy ceiling, I probably would look there first.

The point is, once you get what you want, if you don't want it you change it, and then you go on. You're not stuck continually in that lock of "Oh, do I want that?" and "Can I have that?" because you're on to the next want, to something else that you can have for yourself. Welcome to more life going on.

What Do I Think It Costs?

You know that expression—"I'd give my right arm to have da da da"? Well, I'm not crazy about that expression. You can have your right arm and have what you want, too. You don't have to give up your right arm for what you want. Because if you did give up your right arm for what you want, you certainly wouldn't want it the next time you try to open a mayonnaise jar. Having what you want is not an either-or. You don't have to give up anything to have what you want. The only thing you will give up is what you don't want.

If I Get What I Want, What Will I Have to Give Up?

Do you have acute fear? Do you ask, "What do I lose to get my dream to come true?" Do this: Write on the top of a page in a few words or a short sentence what dream you have in mind for yourself. Be as clear as you can about what it is that you want. Write "I want _____ ." Then write "Do I want _____ ?" with a question mark. Then carry on a conversation with yourself on the page. Chances are that you will probably say yes, you definitely do want this thing, *but*—and then you will say what you fear it will cost you. You start to see all the fears, doubts, and questions that are keeping you from your want.

One thing that will probably come up is that you fear you'll have to do something you don't want to do. As you write, discover what it is that you fear. Say, for instance, that it's the loss of freedom. Then ask yourself, "Well, what is freedom?" And you might answer, "Doing what I want when I want because I want." And as something else comes up, you will start seeing what is keeping you from doing what you want when you want because you want.

What are some of your beliefs? "Well, I won't be a nice person if I do that." "I will hurt somebody else if I do that." All your reasons will present themselves.

A lot of times we're not willing yet to have what we want because we can't see that we can continue to be in control. An example: You want to be chairman of the board, but can you control that? Can you control the whole company? So you keep yourself from being chairman of the board because you don't feel you can have it in your control. The answer is, Let it be out of your control. Allow that there will be more life in your new life and you are willing to go beyond your current control boundaries. When you do that, something quite wonderful happens with freedom, and that is you begin to understand what real freedom is—that you are out of your control and whoopee, you're free to ride on the wave of flow. That's what true freedom is.

See how new experiences expand—not limit. They give us a chance to see what more life there is for us.

So the assignment is to answer the following question with a short sentence: "I want _____ . Do I want _____ ?" Then begin a dialogue with yourself, writing down the things you fear. Now see how that feels in your body. How does it feel in your body when you think your freedom is in jeopardy or you think your nice-guy image is in jeopardy? Then how does it feel in your body when you have what you want? Feel how that feels. Now write a sentence that says you can have both—"I want a job that pays $500,000 and I will have freedom in my job and I will be a nice guy doing this job"—so that you have both things you wish to have, and that *it's not going to cost you one for the other.* And then feel that in your body in its essence. What does that feel like, when both of those are living in you simultaneously, when you have what you want and you don't lose what you fear you'll lose?

P.S. This is abundance.

Will I Get What's Not Good for Me?

If your wish is to make a million dollars and live on an island and be left alone, you won't get it. Because if your wish is to separate yourself from others, you will get the opposite. You will get people in your face *to help you to learn love.* Check now on your wish. Do you want it to flaunt it, to feel superior to others?

If people scare you, the best island for you to live on is the island of Manhattan. Hit it head on.

Seek safety in making peace with your relationships with others. Find out that people don't hurt. Find out that people can love you. Then go live on a tropical island, not as an act of separation, but for the joy of it. Bring friends.

Am I Afraid It Will Change Me?

You want the thing, you really honestly do, but you have some question about whether you can handle the change that's going to happen in your life as a result of having the thing.

Change changes you. If you get what it is that you say you want, it means there are going to be different aspects coming out in your life and you might not like those aspects yet. Compare the feeling to parting with your favorite bathrobe. All your loved ones hate your favorite bathrobe. They will do anything to sneak it out of the house and burn it, but no, you love your favorite bathrobe. You want to stay wrapped in familiarity. You fear that you will lose yourself if you pursue your dream. So what you can do is start to see how (a) you can have familiarity and have the new thing, too, or (b) you can start saying good-bye to your old bathrobe because then that will leave space available for a new bathrobe to come into your life.

Change changes you. It is a time of feeling vulnerable. You want comfort at the very time you need to cultivate openness and willingness. Maybe at this time you don't feel ready to be open and willing.

Ask yourself this: Am I willing to have what I want? Take a piece of paper and talk to yourself about why you are willing to have what you want and all the advantages of having what you want, and find out from that small voice in you, the one that says "I don't wanna, leave me alone, I'm real comfortable where I am and I don't want to move." What's on that little voice's mind? It's really a smart voice and you certainly want to listen to it. It will make all the sense in the world to you. It is also the voice that will then get that part of you ready to have the new thing.

Does Being Right Make Me Happy?

This belief starts very early in life also, when we decide that being right is the next best thing to love. When we are two, we want love. And very often we think that we don't get it. And when we don't get it, we think it must be because of something that we're doing wrong. So every time we try for love and don't get it, we think we're wrong and it sets off a chain reaction. To compensate, rather than going for intimacy, rather than going for love, we go directly for being right. In other words, "It's not my fault; I didn't do it." So then we've shut down all possibilities of love and intimacy.

Watch when people say, "Am I right or am I right?" and they're constantly making a point that they have to be right. It's because early on they felt they were wrong, and that's what closed down the direct path to intimacy.

Can you answer that synapse-breaker question, "Would you rather be right or happy?" Break the knot between them. You were not wrong. You were never wrong. Release yourself from the need to be right. Be free to be happy.

Who's Going to Take Care of Me?

Here's one of the main reasons we don't get what we want: *We want somebody else to get it for us.*

I was called in on a movie project and they asked me, "What do you think is the greatest fantasy that everyone has?" I'm sure they were hoping that I would come up with something salacious, but what I said was, "I think everyone's fantasy is to be taken care of."

Once you can declare that you are the one who can take care of you, then you can ask other people to help. In that way they're taking care of you, but you're the one who's taking care of you by doing the asking. Once you get this straightened out about who takes care of you, then you're free to be taken care of in the manner you wish.

When Is Someday?

Do you have a dream that is way off someplace, for instance, you're going to go to the South Seas *someday*? If somebody gave you air tickets today, would you go? See how you feel about that. See what comes up in terms of putting the brakes on this thing. "Oh no, I don't want to go to the South Seas *today.*" Why? Are you afraid that if you do your someday dream today, you will be done and you'll die? You won't have your someday dream to stay alive for? The South Seas are there now. You can go there now. When you're done, you can go to Toledo.

The Neverending Dream

If you want to have a someday dream and never attain it, that's perfectly fine, too. Be willing to know that, and then you can put it into perspective and then you can shake it down and do the things that are before someday, all those other dreams that are possible that you can have today, right this minute. See how you can start separating one kind of dream from another kind of dream. There are someday dreams, and there's also the dream that is immediate and that is possible and doable, and you don't have to put a someday cost on each of your today dreams.

I Don't Want Anything, That Way I Won't Get Hurt!

Oh, my, this is a deep-seated one and usually comes from very early on. Something happened very, very early in your life when (a) you didn't get what you wanted and (b) you were very deeply hurt by not getting it. Your way to protect yourself from that hurt was to decide to never ever want anything ever again.

This is usually one of the earliest beliefs we acquire, sometimes while still in the womb, and it is usually the last one we uncover in our adulthood. Here is the single most effective antidote: Put your hand over your heart and say, "I can have what I want."

Does What I Have Not Make Me Happy?

I ran into a dear college friend whom I hadn't seen for some time and asked him, "So, what have you been doing for the last fifteen years?" And he said, "Making money." And I said, "Are you a happy boy?" And he said, "No." And I said, "Well, what do you want to do?" And he said "Make more money." He felt that money was supposed to make him happy and, therefore, if he wasn't happy, it was because he hadn't made enough money yet.

There's an easier way. Change your goal. Remember the movie *Rocky*? One of the things we loved so much about Rocky was that about two-thirds into the movie he goes to the arena, it's the night before the fight and the place is . . . oh my gosh, this is a big deal, this is just too big; he's not going to make it. So he comes home to talk to Adrienne, and he sits on the edge of the bed and says, "I can't do this. I'm not going to win this thing," and she says, "Well, what do you want to do, Rocky?" And this is what we love about

Rocky: *He changes his goal!* He says, "I can't win this thing, but I can go the distance," because he knows who he is. He's a ham and egg-er; he's going to be standing no matter how much somebody pummels him. So the rest of the film is Rocky getting pummeled, and in the end he triumphs because he went the distance. He wins because he changed his goal.

Know that it's okay to alter and rearrange and let your plan mature because you get smarter as you go along. When we look, we look with blinders on and can only see two inches in front of our face. As we walk ahead we see more and more of what lies in front of us. With this new knowledge, we get to make new choices. Be open to making those choices and have the plan change as you go. Always let the plan change as you go, because if the plan is rigid, then you might make the plan, but (a) you'll drop dead or (b) you won't be happy with the results. All you will have achieved is completing the plan, which was an illusion in the first place. Be a champ—change your goal and win.

Do I Want the Impossible Dream?

Why do you suppose you want the impossible? Why do you suppose you ask for what is impossible for you to have at this time?

If you have a long-term impossible dream (say you set a goal as a teenager and hope that it pays off in your thirties), you need to ask yourself, "What benefits can I get along the way?" Give yourself results as you go, so that even though you keep working toward the impossible dream, there are increments of success along the way that will be benchmarks for you, that will make you feel as if you're getting there. Hit those stages and phases, and reward yourself lavishly as you go so that you will want to keep going. Otherwise, who would want to? It's no fun.

On your way to an impossible dream, how about giving yourself *possible* dreams? What about all the things that are available to you, that you *can* have, that if you wish for them they could be in your hand within a day or two? Do you set up the impossible for yourself to keep from having any other possible dreams along the way? Are you brave enough to go for the possible along the way? Are you brave enough to have a life now while your impossible dream gets gotten? See what other possibilities there are for you while you take a shot at the impossible.

Now you may say, "But, that's settling for what I don't want." This is a common fear. If you don't get your impossible dream, you fear that what you will do is settle for much less than your ideal. But with Feelization, you can go directly to how you want the impossible dream to make you feel. When you do that, the feeling will give you good, possible ideas to have along the way. If you've set an impossible dream for yourself and don't allow yourself the possible, how is your heart going to know how to play when you finally do let it out to play?

For a moment take the *IM* out of impossible. When you let your ego go, then what was impossible moves over to allow what's possible. IM possible.

The best and fastest way to the impossible dream for tomorrow is to give yourself the possible dreams today.

The Hopeless Hope

There's another, deeper level to the impossible dream. Why do you suppose you want what you can't have? What is the benefit?

If you have impossible dreams now, look at what occurred early in your life. Did your mom die or was your dad very sick? What catastrophic circumstance did you experience early? Chances are that if you have dreams that don't come true now it's because you had a dream that didn't come true then. You learned that dreams don't come true. You just don't know how to let yourself have a dream. You only know how to go directly to loss.

If you dream now and your dream makes you sad, you may be feeling the paradox of hopelessness, for example, "If I keep hoping, maybe my dead daddy will come back. If I give up hope, he'll really be gone." Yes. He's really gone now. Let go of the hopeless hope. When we let go, it's over with and we can have everything else. When we are willing to experience loss, when we are willing to let go of what we want the most, then, for the first time, we will have it. Because the act of letting go eliminates fear of the loss. When we let go of the fear, we can move on to have all our dreams come true.

Can I Let Myself Have the Possible?

Do you think that the only thing that can save you is the Fifty-two Million Dollar Lottery? Here's a story about Murphy's shoes.

A friend of mine took a down-and-out guy, Murphy, to buy a pair of shoes. They shopped for three hours and Murphy couldn't find the right pair. He was looking for shoes that would walk him into a new life. They needed to solve his life. After three hours he ended up with his old falling-apart shoes. Are you Murphy in falling-apart shoes? Would you be willing to see relief in small things?

We all, in one degree or another, get to points when we are so desperate we can't even see the gifts that are there.

It's why a drowning man fights the lifeguard. Lifeguards use a buoy to keep themselves arms-length from whoever they are rescuing so they won't be glommed onto and pulled down, too. It's very hard for a drowning man to trust.

The single way to your impossible dream is trust. The bigger the dream, the bigger the lesson you've set for yourself—to learn trust.

Take a look at your impossible dream. If you set it up to be a tough one to get, that's okay. Say, "I've set it up to be tough to get." Now, be smart. Be willing to receive all the help you can get.

Here's a polarity exercise to do that illustrates the impossible dream. Get out a coin and start flipping it. Just continue to flip it over and over again. See, it comes up heads. See, it comes up tails. This is a polarity, two sides of the coin. What you're wanting to see is all or nothing. Make heads be all. Make tails be nothing. Keep flipping it over and over, and the probability of what comes up all, of what comes up nothing . . . and spin it around and play with the coin and start seeing that there's balance. In an impossible dream, you're dealing with the polarity of "I have to have all because I cannot tolerate nothing," and the having to have it all requires that you are then experiencing the nothing. And what we want you to do is relinquish both parts of the polarity so that you can then experience balance. The reason you're using a coin to do that is because then you will have riches come to you.

■ *The Secret to Having What You Want*

Now that you've explored why you don't get what you want, you get to have a prize. You get to have the Secret to Having What You Want. The all-time Secret to Having What You Want is directly linked to being who you want to be. The more you're doing what you want when you want throughout the day, the more you will have what you want.

Now, you may say, "First I'll get the condo, then I can be myself." Reverse that. Be yourself now. That will get you what you want. You know when you're in situations that you don't feel comfortable, when you have to wear a tie or when you have to say "yes sir, no sir"? You know those situations. We all have been or are currently in them. Those are the ones to begin to start getting out of, because you're not yourself. And when you're not yourself, you're just plain not happy. It's not what you want.

How to Surround Yourself

Make a circle and think of the circle as your day. What percentage of your day are you doing what you want? How much of the day are you who you are? The more you are who you are naturally, the more it is that you are doing what you want, because what you want, fundamentally and deep down, what you want when you want the yacht, when you want the Ferrari, fundamentally and deep down what you want is to be who you are.

You may say, "Pooey, I don't want to be me! I don't even like me! I want to be somebody else!" Well, you are not somebody else. And at the moment you're not the-most-fun-you because you're not appreciating what you have in yourself. Rather than going off to be elsewhere, stay right here with yourself, right where you find yourself now, and work with what you have now. If you feel that you are over-weight and you can't start liking yourself until you lose fifty pounds, guess why you don't lose fifty pounds. If you're going to make major changes in your life, you need to be on your side. And if you are saying that you can love your-self only when you've lost the weight, then you're not on your side. You have to love yourself unconditionally *now*, fifty pounds and all. You can't semi-love yourself now and plan to change it later. Self-love starts first. Be unconditionally crazy about yourself this minute.

PART TWO

How to Get From Where You Are to Where You Want to Be

▪ *Getting It*

All you have to be is who you are. Mostly, we think that we have to get ready, we have to get skills, we have to do this, we have to do that, we're not good enough. To be all that we are is a plenty big enough job. If we just concentrated on that alone, how mighty we would really be. When we are on our own side working one hundred percent to fully be who we are, then who could stop us?

Yes There Is a Better Way

The fastest way out of where you are now is to feel the essence of where you want to be.

You Are What You Feel

To have your heart's desire, go beyond what you can see with your eyes, beyond visualization. Go for the essence. How will it *feel* inside? Feel how it feels to have what you want. When you are willing to go beyond what you think freedom looks like, beyond the familiar, then your want gets gotten.

Remember the blindfold game you played as a kid— "You're getting hot, you're getting cold"? You followed your instincts to your heart's desire. Follow your instincts, and if something doesn't feel right—stop.

Our hearts are smarter than our heads. The heart is the one to follow. And when you follow your heart and let things look different than expected and let it feel good—always let it feel good—it will give you your best result.

This is where the difference between Feelization and visualization comes in. When you are visualizing, you're imagining how you want the result to look, and very often it looks like you're supposed to do a lot of what you don't know how to do. You may think that to get what you want, you have to do something you don't want to do. Pooey. Switch to Feelization and feel good immediately. Feel the essence of what you want. This is a much smarter way to live because it's way more fun and you get what you want.

Let go of what the result is supposed to look like and start feeling how you want it to feel. Be there. Then you can take actions to get there.

A Guide to Life for the Twenty-first Century

The times are changing. Life on earth as we have known it is taking a quantum leap. The earth has speeded up. Have you noticed lately that an hour seems about forty-two minutes long? There's more traffic, more to get done, more emotions, more more more. Do you notice the enormous changes you and everybody around you seem to be going through now? The population has mondo-multiplied. There are lots of us here. There's lots going on. Energy is expanding geometrically.

History Repeats Itself

Do you wonder, "Why is my boss just like my father?"; "Why do all my romances turn out the same?" Patterns are repeating themselves at such a rapid pace that you can't help but notice they are patterns. I like a quote from Edna St. Vincent Millay: "It's not one thing after another. It's the same damn thing over and over again."

We see how our history repeats itself and we want to change. We are changing. The old is falling away. It no longer fits. Many of us are leaving the lives we have been living and yet haven't yet discovered how to live the new way. We are in transition. How do we get from where we are to where we're going? How do we live our lives now to get to our futures?

I'm glad you asked. We've got work to do. We need to look at and get rid of what we carry around that is unacceptable to us. If you've been living with a splinter in your thumb, now suddenly it will start to hurt overmuch so you can pay attention and get rid of it. Many people are experiencing as worse, things that they've been putting up with for so long.

Good-Bye Old Patterns, Hello Better Way

As it feels worse and worse to repeat old patterns, we become less and less tolerant of the same thing over and over. It's as though we've gotten a new snazzy suit and suddenly our old brown shoes need upgrading, too. We're all upgrading our way to be alive.

Energy: An Advanced Course

We are getting lighter in our bodies, and to experience this new light way to be, we have to vacuum out the old stuff. If we choose to stay the same while the world changes, it's not going to feel good. We are reshifting so that we can release old ways of living. We can feel our previously denied fears. We can be free.

Are you asking yourself lately, "What's happening to me?" You may have noticed changes in your body, in your pace, in your food choices, in everything. Feelization can help you open up and lighten up. It can help your personality catch up to how fast you're really going. You can let go of living in the murk and mire and be willing to live light.

Want to?

▪ *Getting Ready*

Take the Step That's There

Do you speak glowingly of the life you want to have and yet you feel stuck where you are? Do you say, "How do I get there?" Do this: Start where you are. If you wait to start where you're not, you're never going to start.

When we want to get from where we are to where we want to be, we think that first we have to get over some terrible bridge to even begin getting there. The terrible bridge is really just our wadded-up hunk of fear that keeps us stuck. Do this: Take the step that is already within your reach. That is the one that will get you there. You will be amazed; the minute you take the small step in front of you, then you'll see the series of small steps that are there and easy to take. Your next step is always within your reach now.

Our journey into our future is not a monumental thing. It's today and it's tomorrow and it's the next day. Ask yourself, "What can I do in a small exquisite way today?" What phone call can you make today that at some point down the line is going to make you your million dollars? I have a client who is a multimillionaire. Guess how he began his empire? He worked on Saturdays. He was a nine-to-five guy, and he added Saturday. He took his Saturday money and built on it. Watch your money become $20 and then $40 and then $80. Build and accumulate and develop and invest and grow with what is available to you at this time.

Watch successful people. They will show you that they haven't got any more natural resources than you've got. What they do is *use* their resources. Look at your phone. What can you do to get money on the line? You can pick up a phone and you can make a phone call, and maybe you're not very good at it, but you can begin. Maybe you're not very good at it, but you'll do it anyway, and then maybe you'll get better at it, and then maybe you'll get a little result, and then maybe you'll get a better result.

The next step is always there, it is always within you, and it's always waiting and available for you to take action on it at any moment when you are ready. There's nothing more that you need to take the next step that is there.

How Do I Go Beyond Where I Always Stop?

I just got a call from a client. She's done it again: she's managed single-handedly to write, produce, direct, and sell a major TV network on her project. She's miraculous.

Except she wasn't calling to celebrate. She was calling frantically because she doesn't know below-the-line budgeting. She's already achieved the impossible; now the easy part stops her cold. She looks and sees only what skills she doesn't have.

Do you stop when you get to the end of your familiar territory? Do you feel that you can't go on to new ground? Do this: Look at what you can do and offer that. Value what you do have. You are enough at this very moment. Go with what you have and not be stopped by what you don't have.

When you go with what you already have, you'll get more. As you get really happy about taking the small step that's there, quantum leaps occur.

The way to be an expert at your future is by taking the step that's there today.

Making It Up as You Go Along

Making it up as you go along is the only way that life occurs. We may think that we make very clever plans for ourselves, but how life works is that we make it up as we go along whether we think we do or not.

I work with students at USC, and just before graduation they, of course, have that horrendous feeling about "Oh my gosh, real life is going to happen June tenth, and I have to know what I'm going to do." That's what real life is for, to let you find out what you'll do. You don't have to know it beforehand. By the way, real life is happening all the time for all of us, whether or not we've graduated.

The Nearsightedness of Farsighted Projection

When you're having a conversation with yourself, does it often go something like this:

SELF

I'll buy the lottery ticket and make a million dollars and leave Paducah for Hollywood and be famous and go to all the parties and meet starlets and have a high life, but it will be empty of meaning and I'll get disillusioned and lose all my money and have to come home and the town folks will laugh at me and I'll be ruined with no hope but to buy a lottery ticket and make a million dollars and. . . .

This is projection. You live your future in fear before you even get there. It has no value to your present moment. It most especially has no value to your future moments in which you will be different than you are today. Take life a step at a time as you go.

You may say, "What, don't plan?" Look around at how you'd like it to feel. See alternatives and choices that are possible for you down the line. That's perfectly fine. That's what you're doing this minute. You don't have to live your future now. You know the song, "Life Is What Happens to You While You're Making Other Plans"? Well, watch your life and what's happening in it. If you see that you are heading for jail, then you can change your behavior now in this moment. Backtrack from your future thought to your present behavior and see, "I have a choice here; I could not rob this bank."

If you have a future vision, then lay track to it now at the present moment and make it up as you go along. In *Raiders of the Lost Ark,* at the height of jeopardy Marian turns to Indiana Jones and says, "What are you going to do?" And he says, "I don't know, I'm making this up as I go along." Because in fact that morning he could not have put on his Do list "Blow up plane, duck all the bullets." What he did do that morning was put on his Indiana Jones hat and have his bullwhip with him. In other words, what we bring to the present moment of life are our personalities, our dexterities, our skills, our confidences, our experiences, our hearts. And those qualities then formulate the next moment and the next moment, and when you are making it up as you go along, it becomes a wonderful action-adventure!

So How's Your Wattage Working?

I watched an anxious mother on the beach make a picnic lunch for her kids. She put all her accident fears into spreading peanut butter on the bread.

How much wattage are you putting into each task you do? Notice when you're driving. Do you have white knuckles? Is your body tight? Why? Why do we do that? My theory is that we are running wattage equal to our thoughts rather than equal to the task at hand.

While you are driving, if you are thinking of what you have to do when you get to the office, you may have a hundred-watt job on your mind. As you think about it, you burn one hundred watts behind the wheel. This is emotional wattage. Would you like to be energy-efficient with your emotions? Notice when you're throwing big watt energy into something that could have a much lighter touch to it. For instance, when you're driving, lean back, loosen up, let your leg muscles relax. You'll notice that you can give ten watts to the job of driving instead of one hundred watts, and then you won't burn out.

The Body Electric

Let's look at your wattage. Think of it like a neon coil, a Frankenstein zzzt-zzzt kind of laboratory coil that runs through the center of yourself. Think of it up and down your spine. Take a look at how much energy you're running through your coil. How does it feel? Take a deep breath, move around, jiggle your insides, loosen up. See how little energy you can send through the coil. See how much you can send. Play around with how big the push up the coil can be. How much light can you make it radiate? Does the brightness take more effort or less effort? Be energy-efficient. Can you experience more with less effort? See and feel the range of possibilities. Feel the different ways that it feels in your body.

Congratulations! You're aware of doing this now. You will remember the next time you make a hundred-watt peanut butter sandwich. You have a choice. You can lighten up on the wattage or use the wattage to go build a skyscraper.

Amping Up for End Product

See what's a ten-watt job, what needs fifty watts, what's a hundred-watt activity. Feel the coil inside you and feel how you can run the energy that is equal to the task at hand. Once you master specific wattage, you can take a look at how you use sweeping energy.

What Is Sweeping Energy?

Did you ever pack to go to Toronto when suddenly, at the last minute, you absolutely must fix the zipper on your jacket you haven't worn since high school?

When we need our circuits to blast full out in one area, we often create a sweeping energy from another area. That's why the floor never gets scrubbed until taxes are due. We are amping up all around to sweep the area we want to bring from nothingness to beingness. Our electrical system knows that something always comes of something.

Note how it feels when you pump up to get a task done. And note how it feels when you use specific wattage for the task. Actually choose when to use which method.

Willing It into Being

One of the things you'll find when you're wishing desperately for something is that you tend to run a lot of energy through your coil over and over again. "Oh, I want that. Oh boy, I really want it." Meanwhile, the thing requires that you only run the wish once and then let it go. For instance, when you write a letter to Santa Claus, if you keep writing the letter saying "I want this and I want this and I want this" and you never mail the letter, Santa Claus is just not going to get it. What you want to do is say "I want this—period. Thank you very much." Send it out. Let what you want come back to you.

When you play with this coil, begin to feel how much effort a thing really needs. Amazingly, most things need very little. Cultivate a light touch. For instance, if you want a career as a famous actress, you might say, "Oh, I want this, I want this, I want this," and you're hoping hard and you run big watt energy, and then you don't get it. And then because you don't get it, you run even bigger watts. Unrelenting wattage. It's not that you're not doing enough. It's that you're doing too much. The energy part works, and you've done it. Now *let it go*. Drop it through, from thought to reality; mail the letter; mail the wish to Santa Claus. Now roll up your sleeves and take the next action in front of you and the next and the next.

If Energy Is Unlimited, Why Am I So Tired?

If you feel tired, sleep. That's what feeling tired is for—to tell you to rest. It's okay. Once you start sleeping, you'll be amazed at how tired you really are. It's okay. Rest some more. Something's working itself out. Let it. Something's taking a whole lot of energy. *That* is why you're tired—not because you don't have energy.

If you are not able to take good care of yourself at the moment, if you're having any imbalance in your life, it will take your energy. It's not that you have no energy, it's that you're using tremendous energy to hold back a twelve-ton locomotive. Ask yourself, "What's taking my energy?"

I'll give you a hint. You're usually tired when you are forcing yourself, against your will, to do something that you don't want to do. What is it you're doing that you don't want to do? If you can't get up in the morning to go to a job you don't like, then the problem is not that you're tired—the problem is the job.

When you stop fighting yourself, your self won't have to resist you. Have your whole self work together and you'll see how much energy you have to work out the problem.

The Positive-Negative Bad News Polka

Do you think you absolutely have to do more, be more, have more now? Do you think that who you are and what you do isn't enough? Do this:

1. Write the word "negative" on a small piece of paper.
2. Write the word "positive" on another piece of paper.
3. Thank them for being in your life, then tear them both up and throw them in the air. Now go on, free of them.

How to do this: Here's what I learned from living at the ocean. There's tide in and tide out. Neither is positive or negative. Circumstances have ebb and flow aspects to them. Some months you have more money than other months. Some days you're more in love with your loved ones than other days. If you're willing to see this and allow the natural ebb and flow, you save yourself lots of anguish about how you're going to force it otherwise.

Shoulds

Write down a speed list of all the things you "should" do today. Ready? Go. Examples:

I should lose 125 pounds and marry a movie star.

I should be a movie star myself.

I should clean up the garage.

I should do the report my boss wanted last August.

Now, look at the list. Are most of them what your mind decided would be the right thing? How many are "feel goods," because you feel like doing them? Notice the difference between the ideas from your mind and the ideas from your heart. Do most of them come from the critical take-care-of-business part of yourself? Do you notice the voice you use with the should list? Is it stern, serious, scolding?

Here's the truth about should lists: They're hard jobs you don't feel like doing, and once you force yourself to do them, all they are is done and you have to face more tomorrow.

Here is something I learned about myself: Wild horses can't get me to do what I don't want to do. And wild horses can't stop me from doing what I feel like doing. Once I learned that, I'm soooooooo much happier. I don't fight myself. I know you have the same wild horses in your life. Forgive yourself for not doing what you don't feel like doing. Enjoy yourself by doing what you *do* feel like doing.

Here's how: If you have a should list you make every day, it's guaranteed that you won't get everything on the list done. So what you've got are intentions, and those keep you in-tension all day. Not the happiest way to live. Do this: If you must make out a list, change it from a "Things to Do" list to a "How I Want to Feel" list. For instance, you have on your should list to paint the bedroom and every night you go in there and hate yourself for not doing your should. Today approach it this way: Ask yourself, "How do I want to feel in the bedroom?" Now feel it. Sink deeply into the bed, cozy and pleased with yourself. Suddenly you will know what would help. Maybe you don't need to paint. Maybe you need to move the dresser so you don't bump your shin.

Here's a big all-time important secret to the happiness of life: Whatever you're not doing you're not doing for a very good reason. Great. Don't do it. Honor yourself for not doing it. Be free.

P.S. Using this method you will get more done than you have ever gotten done before, and you'll be happier doing it because you've moved out of being in-tension and replaced it with spontaneous action on what you really want.

"But," you might say, "I have an obligation. I have a family to feed. I have to do what I don't want to do." We all have priorities. Okay, you want the house for the family so you'll go to work to pay for it. No one said you have to be miserable doing that. I take that back. Somebody must have said to you, "You have to be miserable doing it." Maybe your father went to work as his obligation to take care of his family and you hated that he hated it, and now you're doing it to yourself and your family.

Commitment Is to Yourself

You have an obligation to give yourself happiness because that permeates to all around you. Do your part to have it feel good to you, and everybody around you will feel good, too.

Why We Are Impatient
and What to Do About It—Immediately

Were you ever in a restaurant and your food didn't come and didn't come? Maybe you were patient and waited. Finally you said, "Where's my hamburger?" And the waitress said, "Oh, did you want a hamburger?" Now you're really mad. You're mad at her, and you're also mad at yourself for believing that your hamburger was forthcoming.

So the problem with patience is not always patience. The problem is trust. Is what you're waiting for really on its way? If it isn't on its way, the action to take is not waiting for it to get there. Instead, the action to take is get the thing rolling in your direction.

When you are impatient, take a look. You might be very smart here. There's a subpersonality in you telling you that another job needs doing.

No Such Thing as Waiting

Notice when you've done everything to generate what you want and it's coming. Notice how relaxed you get. Notice how patient you are about its arrival. That's because you know it's coming and you're not waiting, you're actually getting ready. There's never such a thing as waiting, because if you wait, life will go on without you.

Attitude

Do you have a friend who's slim and her children are talented and they go on fun vacations and she never has a headache? Usually we all have in our lives people whose lives are working when ours aren't, and when we look at them we don't like them a bit.

Well, watch those people as if they are blessings. They do have problems. They don't have it all smooth all the time. And if you'll watch, you'll notice that what they also have is a great attitude. They have an ability to enjoy what is occurring. If they don't like what's going on, you usually will hear about it in an honest way when they're working it out, when they're finding ways to make changes while being willing to be honest about what is going on. They don't deny the feeling. They have the feeling and don't judge the feeling while they are making changes beyond the feeling.

If you have such happy people in your life, by all means the best way to have them in your life is to delight in them and to watch and learn ways you too can get out of recurring and old patterns you may be stuck in. Watch how someone faces up and extrapolates the delights in life and carries on.

Also, look at what's an issue to you. If you are overweight, make a friend with somebody who is slim. Find where your issue lies. If you are overweight and you see someone slim, you might say, "Oh, I hate her because she's slim." See what you're really saying. Are you saying, "I hate her because she's slim and I'm not, and if she's slim and I'm not, then who I really hate is me"? Now begin to forgive yourself because it's okay that you're not slim. It's perfectly fine. That's what you are. And so then if you can forgive yourself for that, then you can begin to start looking at your slim friend and see how she chews.

Am I Enough?

You may ask, am I enough? You are *God*! You are all. Of course you're enough. If anything, you're too much. Be cool. Lighten up. Let go. Enough's enough.

Not-Enoughness

The number one single most overriding painful dilemma of humans is that they don't think they're good enough. You can see this not-enoughness problem in others easier than in yourself. It's very easy to spot it any day of the week on any street. Most humans suffer from chronic not-enoughness. The way to spot it is when someone gives you something you didn't ask to get. They will want to give you a piece of themselves for safekeeping and love. They are asking, "Won't you please regard me, respond to me, see my value, love me? That's what I so want to give to you." You will say, "Out of my way."

This gives fuel to two fires—theirs: "Oh, I'm not good enough," and yours: "Maybe I can be good enough because I'm better than they are." And once more an exchange has occurred to separate us from one another.

You'd be amazed at how good-enough you start to feel when you appreciate that others are good-enough where they are. Try going to a party, such as your high school reunion and not judge how you are in comparison to others. If all the energy that went into us humans comparing ourselves to one another, if all that energy were bottled, we wouldn't need another drop of fossil fuel to run the Western world.

Here's a funny story about this fear of not stacking up good-enough to other human beings: I picked up a writer colleague to go to a big deal network story conference. We were meeting with what is commonly referred to as a "suit," which is an executive with "yes" power. Carol was very nervous and when we arrived at the hotel suite, she looked down and noticed that she had a tiny moth hole in her skirt. Well, my dear friend, who by the way looked perfectly beautiful, became a screeching zoo primate in the hallway. She was sure this moth hole meant that we weren't going to get the writing assignment, that she would be banished from Hollywood forever, that she was never going to get any work ever again. It was a classic attack of not-good-enoughness. Well, we went into the hotel suite of this big hotsy-totsy suit she thought would judge her, would look down upon her as not-good-enough. We went in there, and he was another zoo primate! He said he was so nervous about meeting us that he took a Valium, and then he took a drink and they didn't mix and then, there before us, he passed out. To my knowledge he never did notice Carol's moth hole.

So, if you are concerned with "are you enough," yes, yes, you are—always. And so is everybody you encounter.

Hot Ballooning in the Garage

Are you asking for something that you really don't want? Pay close attention to your fantasies. Do you really want a beautiful blonde woman to appear one night to help you with your socks? Some wishes we want to be arm's length away to excite us, but not involve us.

My friend Helen said she always dreamed of being an important Hollywood producer who would have glamorous celebrity-laced pool parties at her Bel Air mansion where she would wear gold lamé shoes and be scintillating. I asked her if in this fantasy she was wearing a sun hat. She said no. And I thought that was all very interesting since Helen has the fairest skin in the land and never goes in the sun without a hat. She has also never, to my knowledge, ever worn gold lamé shoes. Further, she *is* influential and quite powerful in Hollywood, and people would come to her parties if she ever had them—but she hates parties, she never has them, and she never even goes to any. So what is this gold lamé dream?

Look at what the real wish is that is underneath it all. Helen, in her dream, really is wishing that she were a different person than she is. A part of her wants to be rich, powerful, fashionable. When she saw herself at her party she saw the *essence* and the *feeling* of what she wanted to have. She wanted that confidence and joie de vivre that such a person would have, and she attached that to gold lamé shoes. She really didn't want gold lamé. She wanted what she associated with gold lamé, which was simply a good feeling about herself. But associating it with gold lamé caused her to think it was unattainable and not really desirable.

To Get What You Want, You Don't Have to Wish for What You Don't Want

Ask yourself this: What are my fantasies telling me about what I want in my reality? What do I admire about myself in my daydreams? Do I have these qualities now and can I cultivate these qualities now in my life? The way to use Feelization is that you can capture the essence of what it is your fantasies are telling you and feel it in your body, feel how it feels to have the gold lamé party. Then identify the qualities that you really want. Clarify what your symbols represent, and then you don't have to get the symbols outside yourself. You can feel the feeling you want to feel immediately inside yourself. Confidence is self-given. It's an inside quality. You don't have to buy it at a shoe store.

Dreams You Hope Don't Come True

Our fantasies come to us to give us great information about what we want in essence. Once we get the picture, we are free to not carry out the fantasy. For instance, you would love to tell everybody that you've experienced riding in a hot air balloon, but the truth is you really don't want to get up at dawn and drive three hours to stand in a basket and float across the countryside at great personal risk to your beloved body parts. You would, however, love to sit in the living room of your friends and be able to speak of the experience. So look at some fantasies you have in that light—that there are some things you would like to have done, but you don't really ever want to do them.

▪ *Being Love*

There Is More to Love Than We Know

People love you how they want to love you, not necessarily how you want to be loved. A happy heart is one that's willing to receive how it is loved, not require the love to be for certain reasons.

If you have a small hole in your heart that you are trying to fill, stop trying to fill it from the small hole. Here's an example: Maybe you wanted your father's approval when you were a teenager. You're at the breakfast table, and you begin to grouse, and he begins to grouse back. The channel that you have opened between you is about ten watts. And you're sending out ten watts of hope to him through this small hole in your heart. You want desperately to have his approval. So you're sending out this wound, this hole in your heart. He's sending back on that same line of wattage because that's all you're sending out. Exactly what you're giving out, which is ten watts, is what you are receiving back, which of course is not adequate to fill the small hole in your heart.

Hearts are much bigger than that. And love is much bigger than that. And you know that. You want the big love. You don't want this ten percent. But if you are opening up only that ten-watt hole to receive in, then it can't possibly give you enough back, so instead of feeling love, you feel not-enoughness.

Picture a beautiful, healthy, magnificent heart that's beating and throbbing. You need to have love come radiating, sunshining into your whole throbbing heart.

There is more to love than we presently allow ourselves to experience.

Are you waiting to love until somebody loves you? How will you know what love is until you give it away?

The Do Nothing Approach to Love

You don't have to work at being loved. People love you in spite of what you do for love, not because of it.

I have a client who thought he was loved for constantly putting himself through a hero's journey, blazing trails, walking boldly through crisis. But no matter how big the brave act, he still didn't get enough love, so he did more and more. His loved ones didn't love him for that. If they did, he'd have to keep doing it to get love. People loved him enough to *not* love him for that. Finally he got it. He can stop doing that and be loved "as is." He doesn't have to *do* anything for love.

You're Doing It On Purpose

Where you are is where you want to be. If you feel you haven't yet gotten what you want, know that there is a greater want inside that is keeping you where you are. Here's an example: A boy grows up and his father has been unfaithful to his mother. There is extraordinary emotion and anguish associated with this knowledge that connects him to his parents; he hates his father, he protects his mother, he hates his mother—he feels all sorts of conflicts. Often, men in their thirties try to reconcile how they go forward in their lives separate from their parents. Many find themselves being unfaithful to their spouses. They loathe this in themselves because they loathed it in their fathers. Why is it that they are unfaithful? It is an act of love, it is their way of remaining connected to their fathers by having history repeat itself.

When we understand that we do what we do on purpose, then we can uncover why we do what we do. It is always an act of love. And once we uncover what we are doing for love we are free to understand what love really is. Love is not suffering, love is not sacrifice, love is not being loyal to a family behavior that does not serve your best interest.

Our wants are fundamentally linked to how we understood love from an early age.

Whatever you are doing, presently, you are doing it as a metaphor. What you are really doing is going through the labyrinth of how you were loved as a child.

How to Create a Love Scene Starring You

People who feel successful as adults are those who have childhood memories of being loved. No matter what tragedies or poverties or whacks across the face they had, they also have the ability to come up with a kind of high grade from childhood where they remember the love scenes.

Now I'm not saying that their childhoods were any more elegant than yours. And I'm not saying that they aren't denying any difficulties in their childhoods. But if you can go back and find some moment of recollection of love, those are powerful keys to being satisfied as an adult.

Past Perfect

Do you remember being loved as a child? Here's an exercise: Sit down, close your eyes, and press your rerun button. Go back to your early life and see what pops out as a moment of love from early times.

When one memory pops up, it's usually connected to a string of love memories that you didn't even know were there. Surprise and comfort yourself today, as you discover that your dad really did say he loves you. Love memories from long ago can give you a good idea about how to feel about yourself today.

Stuff these new love pictures into your memory wallet to carry around with yourself now. Have them replace the separation pictures you have been carrying. Go ahead, reinvent your childhood.

Past Imperfect

You may say, "Fine, I want to but I can only see sad scenes or fearful scenes." Then what is the theme here?

What string of scenes are coming up? Do they all themat-
ically have the same feel to them? As an adult, you can now
change these scenes. You can go back and replay them and
change the endings. What is the outcome you want? How
would you have it happen? Do that now.

What Time Is It?

What you're doing is playing with time frame. In past
perfect, you are going back and being your past and allowing your past to come to your present and bring love to it.
In past imperfect, you are here, in the present, then you
are going back to the past and changing it from the present. And here's a third method to play with. Go to your
future. Put yourself in tomorrow or twenty years from now,
and feel how it feels to be who you will become. Find that
in your body and find how different you will feel in your
body then. As your future-self, go back to your past-self and
heal your past from your future. Welcome to the present.

Having a Love Affair with Yourself

Are you looking for Mr. or Ms. Right? Do you feel, "If only I can find my perfect mate, then I'll have this love category solved"? If you look at what you desire in a lover, you can really get clarity on what you would love to see in yourself. Many a young woman is looking for a man who is rich and handsome, has a good career and a sense of humor and who will take care of her. If you look at what you want in him, you might see that some of those traits are what you really want in yourself. The way your subconscious is thinking of getting those things for yourself is by marrying them, when in essence you really want to acquire those kinds of abilities and qualities within yourself. That's why you don't find this guy—because he's not who you really want. You really want this for yourself. You are Mr. or Ms. Right for you.

Try this the next time you're between soul mates. Have a love affair with yourself. All that you wish to have outside yourself, cultivate within yourself. If you want somebody who can pick the restaurant, *you* read the restaurant reviews and pick the restaurant. Take yourself to a movie and enjoy your own company. Be fascinated with yourself. Until you can have a love affair with you, you can't begin to have as much fun as there is with somebody else.

Love Is a Monologue

One of my clients is a young man new at love. He was pining deeply over the breakup with his first major girlfriend. He said, "It just didn't work out." And I said, "What makes you think it didn't work out?" It was fun to watch it dawn on him that he had learned so much and most of what he had learned was *because* of breaking up, and so it did "work out."

I have a theory about the current global interest in soul mates. We encounter soul mates by the minute—the checker at the grocery store who remembers our radishes, the driver at the stoplight who smiles just as we're plotting mayhem. We have the idea that love means happily every after—no lessons, no changes, fixed and set. Hearts are living organisms; they grow and change. Relationships will cause us to grow whether we want to or not.

The most asked question to love advisers must be, "Is this the one? Is she my soul mate? What's going to happen with her and me and this and that?" What's going to happen is that you're going to learn some love lessons, and it may be rocks and arguments and you want it to be hearts and flowers, and this is the person you learn your love lessons with at the moment. Your lover loves you enough to be a mirror for you, and the very things you don't want and say you fear and will not abide are what you seem to attract through this loved one. And it's okay. A stranger wouldn't bother to give you this hard a time.

I Did Everything Right
and Still It Turned Out Wrong

There is a difference between self-punishment and responsibility.

If you blame yourself and come down really hard on yourself and criticize yourself, then you might notice that you also swing to the other side and indulge yourself. You might find that you have both swings, being extremely conscientious and then being extremely self-punishing, both extremes.

We touched a bit on this topic in the section "Do I Try and Still Not Get What I Want?" Do you have a pattern of working, working, working and then dropping? And do you find yourself saying, "I tried; it just didn't work. I tried everything. I did everything right and still it turned out wrong." Do you notice this is extremely painful, this is horrible, it's so hard on you? And it's hard on you for none of the apparent reasons.

If you think, "I work hard and sacrifice and do more than anybody else and then it still doesn't work out," what's going on here is this: You're needing to be off the hook. You're needing to feel that it's not your fault.

I have a dear former student David. He's on the brink of living in his car because he can't stand to have another junk job. Well, he's right. He needs to not have another junk job. But he isn't yet ready to hear that he's off the hook from having a junk job. He just keeps going on interview after interview so he can say, "See, they're not hiring. See, I'm overqualified. See, it's not my fault." He wants everyone to say to him "You can't have this junk job" because that is his dearest wish. He does not want a junk job, but he's not yet ready to take the responsibility of saying that he doesn't. So, I have said to David, "Stop it. If you refuse to have a junk job, then stop applying for them." Eventually he will be able to say, "I don't have to punish myself." Then he can go on to "I am responsible for myself."

See how self-punishment gets you nowhere. And it hurts! When you find that you are in a spin of "Well, I've tried and I've tried" and nothing works, say this, say this loud and clear, put your hand over your heart and say, "It's not my fault; it's not my fault." Say it over and over again. Because, the deal is, it's not your fault. You are off the hook. Get off the hook, and then you are free to start being responsible.

Now, if it's not your fault, why do you want to punish yourself? In David's case, he's a talented concert pianist, and when he was a child his mother told him that he would never make a living as a concert pianist and that he would have to have just a menial job. So here he is at 40 years old, up to his neck in menial jobs and he can't go on any longer with that. Finally it's time for him to say no to his mother's belief. He has required everyone to say no to him until he becomes ready to switch from self-punishment to being responsible. Until he is ready to finally say yes to the life that he wants to have, he remains in this self-punishment.

What's the way out of this one? Well, you want to be treated better. However people are treating you, it's because you expect it to be that way. If you want to be treated better, treat yourself better. That is the difference. Lavish yourself, appreciate yourself, accept yourself. That is your responsibility. Stop self-punishment.

Be Your Own Grown-Up

Learn to be a great parent to yourself. If your parent told you something that now, as an adult, is not working in your life, then you can now be the parent to yourself and change that belief. Actually parent the part of you that is still an infant. Give yourself a lollipop after your chores. Decide on a treat somewhere between a Ferrari and an ice cream cone that you can afford, and give that to yourself. Be a loving parent.

If you have lots of money but you never treat yourself, really cut loose and splurge very big. If you are an over-spender, then find cheap thrills, find ways that you can give treats to yourself that don't require money. Give yourself a lovely walk in nature.

Being a great parent to yourself is the surest way to elim-inate self-punishment and to take responsibility. It's the lit-tle things. Do you often have headaches? Headaches are not natural. They are not there to be "aspirined." They're there to show you that there is something in your life that needs remedying. Is it at a particular time of day when you get a headache? Is it after you pick up your kids from day-care, or before supper when there's nothing in the refriger-ator because you didn't have time to food shop? Locate in what way you are not being treated well. Locate where and when that occurs, and remedy the situation. If your child always had a headache, you'd take care of it. Do the same for yourself.

Pay yourself first. Pay yourself first physically. Do you have a phone answering machine? Do you run in the house when you get home because you have to go to the bath-room? Which do you do first, go to the bathroom or listen to your answering machine? Go to the bathroom, then lis-ten to the phone messages. Your body comes first! Your first responsibility is to yourself physically. Take care of you. If you don't take care of you, you're not going to be efficient for taking care of anything else. That's the first responsi-bility. If you need food, eat. If you're tired, sleep.

On an airplane at takeoff, we're all instructed that if we have small children, we should put the oxygen on ourselves first and then the children because if we're out cold we're not any good to ourselves or our children. So always pay yourself first. That is how you have plenty to give.

The Myth of the Unbreakable Heart

Many of us have a goal. We want more than anything else in the world to get to the place where we're not going to have any problems anymore, where things are not going to affect us, where we're going to have eternal bliss, enlightenment, and a balanced bank account forever after.

I'll tell you the secret of how to do this. The secret of an unbreakable heart is not to protect it and secure it and separate it and make it hard or impervious. The secret is to open it.

The only kind of heart that doesn't break is an open heart. How do you have an open heart? This is so simple. Here's how: When you have a feeling, feel it no matter what the feeling is. That's it, because the feeling *is* there, and you are feeling it. The pain comes in when you do anything to not feel it. You will do everything to keep it down, to deny it, if it's a feeling you don't like. But the feeling is there anyway, so go ahead and feel it. Feelings felt aren't nearly as terrible as feelings denied.

In fact, do you notice that once you feel your feelings you're so relieved? "Oh, is that all that feels like? I can handle that." Once you feel the feelings, you know that feelings don't kill you—it's *not* feeling them that does all the damage.

So the deal is, feel the feelings. Now, what about all those trap doors that have been shut between the original feeling and the open air, feelings that are all closed down in the inner sanctum, in the sub-subbasement of our bodies? We want to get all those feelings out and have all those doors open, and the only thing that comes in then is fresh air.

You may say, "Fresh air? Are you kidding? I have to close down; I have to protect myself. I can't be out there with an open heart! My gosh, I'll die!"

Here's a wonderful mechanism that occurs in the human body: We won't open until we have the capacity to handle what is there for us. We have tremendous capabilities for protecting ourselves. If we didn't, we wouldn't be here. We're masters at protection. That's enough. We don't need to be extra-masterful at protection. We can take care of the other end of the balance.

See how your heart has been shut. Do you separate and isolate and protect your heart so that it won't get hurt? Are you getting very, very good at building a brick wall around your heart? Do you notice that you can still get hurt? Do you notice that the brick wall keeps out the sunshine, the possibility, the nourishment that your heart needs so it can be resilient and it can be strong in such a way that it can roll with the punches?

Do this exercise now: Very quickly, write down maybe five beliefs you find you have with "If I open my heart, then _____ ." Fill in the blank with five different ideas, like "If I open my heart, I'll get hurt"; "If I open my heart, someone will take advantage of me." That kind of thing. Do you see a pattern here? Do you see what particular arrow you protect your heart from?

Track what you keep your heart closed to. You were right to do it. You were right to do it because you needed that protection. And now you're going to start being aware of what you're protecting yourself from. When you're aware of it, you can begin to heal it.

Are You Pleasing Others at the Expense of Yourself?

Do you serve the steak to everybody else and eat the fatty part yourself? That is not healthy. It is not healthy for you; it is not healthy for the others whom you want to please because it holds them in obligation, which is exactly why you might be doing it in the first place. Give it up.

Change the Course of Your History

Stop treating yourself the way you don't want to be treated. Always treat yourself the best way you can.

Ask yourself this: Who is my priority? (The answer is, *you* are your priority.) Take care of yourself first; that takes care of everyone else. This applies even if you're a parent. (You know that when you have taken care of yourself first the kids get along with you better.)

Never please others at the expense of yourself. It costs too dearly, to them and to you and to all concerned, and it just doesn't work. And it isn't any fun at all. Nobody likes it. So stop it.

Taking the Not-Been-Thanked-Enough
Part of You to Dinner

If you don't appreciate what you already have, you can't have any more.

If you want more, practice appreciating what you have. Appreciating what you have gets you much more. If you find yourself saying, "Oh pooey, my life is doggey-doo, I didn't do this, I don't have that," immediately call a friend and meet for dinner. Meet at the hotsy-totsiest restaurant you can find, and what you need to do when you get there is to completely celebrate what you *do* have, and honor and toast all the accomplishments that you have achieved, and recognize and remember and reminisce about where you were and how you got out of those messes, how you've surmounted those obstacles and that you are so much better off now than you were.

When you take your not-been-thanked-enough parts to dinner, appreciate yourself! All the topics of conversation appreciate your tremendous accomplishments and appreciate where you came from. You're not allowed to belly-ache or to say anything terrible about anybody else and what they're not doing that you want them to do so that your life would be better. Just thoroughly enjoy who you are.

There's a curious, wonderful thing that happens at such a dinner. At first some belly-aching will want to come up, and then you will find a higher thought to tell instead, and as you progress through the dinner you start to see that you've got some new ideas. Without even talking about problems you think you have in your life, suddenly good ideas will come to you to solve those problems. But you are not talking about the problems; what you are talk-ng about is what you've already achieved, what you are talking about is new skills you've already acquired, and the main thing is for you to see how far you've come. You've come a long way, baby! And now you really recognize that. One of the great joys in being alive is when you can connect one thought to another thought and one occurrence to a behavior that you have, and you begin to start seeing how everything is connected. That is love, and it gets you all the more.

So when you start doing the not-been-thanked-enough dinners, you start to see yourself catch up to how far you've come. Appreciate yourself! Meet a friend once a month or once a week to appreciate yourself. When you look with new eyes, you start appreciating and you begin seeing the enormity of things you've learned and ways you are doing things in a better way, changing patterns and being much more aware.

And you can have dessert if you want to. . . .

How to Be Yourself

When I was a really little kid I was going to tap dance in a show and I was all nervous about it. I must have been five years old, and my mother said to me, "Just be yourself." Well, I was five—who was myself? For all of us between five and somewhere in midlife, I hope we've developed a real knack for being ourselves. And if we find that self in situations when we're not expressing who we are, if we're pretending or restricting or masking ourselves in some way, those are all the places that we aren't doing what we want because we aren't being who we are.

Now, what to do about that? Express yourself in those situations when you aren't expressing yourself, and if you can't express yourself in those situations, then stop being in those situations. Very simple, like Steve Martin's joke (How to make a million dollars and not pay taxes—first, make a million dollars). The more you pay attention to when you're not being who you are or not being heard, the more those situations will change. You don't change the situation. You change one small thing in yourself. And then change happens spontaneously. That's the key. If we think we need to change the thing outside ourselves, then the thing doesn't get changed because it's very big and impossible. If we know it's the other way around, that we change something in ourselves, that we allow ourselves to express ourselves more genuinely and more honestly and we follow our hearts and use our instincts and are open and willing to show who we really are instead of who we think we should be, then we become much happier.

I heard a wonderful anecdote about Oliver Nelson, who was a prominent, talented musician and composer. In his early times when he was creating his music and struggling to pay the bills, he became a bus driver. He was not a happy bus driver; he couldn't handle it. He stopped the bus in the middle of the street and just got out and left the bus. Pretty amazing!

Now, I don't mean that you should run right out and abandon your bus in the middle of the road at rush hour, but I'm using this story as an illustration of a basic truth: Listen to your heart. When it's screaming to get out of a situation, don't deny it; listen to it and take action. Oliver's action might have been quite radical, but if he had not taken it, then what? He had to follow his heart. He did become prominent and sought-after as a film composer. Somewhere between hating your junk job and doing what you love, find your commitment to follow your heart.

A Kinder, Gentler You

This is a good place to talk yet again about denial. If you aren't following your heart, then what you're doing is arguing with it or denying it. And denial hurts. Denial builds up in your body because you're denying what your body wants and what it needs. And if you are denying a problem, then you take the denial and play it out in your body. You play out the denial in your body because you're not listening to it with your heart. So your body has to say, "Okay, you're not listening with your heart? So then we'll amplify it by giving you a headache." This is quite exquisite and it's quite complicated and what you're doing is quite on purpose.

When we deny our emotional needs, our emotional needs will plug into the amp of our entire bodies so that we can hear it louder and clearer. If we won't listen when it's a small voice, it will amp way up and tell us with the speakers that are turned on all through our bodies. We'll be told with a headache or ulcer or cancer. Yipes!

Facing Up to the Down Side

The answer to denial of course is to face up, to acknowledge what's going on. And by acknowledging what's going on, you no longer deny the needs your body has. Once you acknowledge that you are in a situation you don't like, you can then work with what you have been denying. If you're in an untenable situation, then you've got to get out of there, otherwise what you are doing is being untenable to yourself. You've taken the situation and you've lodged it in your body.

Simple. (Don't you love when I say "simple"? It's when the hardest part always comes.) Acknowledge what you've denied. And when you acknowledge what you've denied, floodgates open and in rush all the actions that you can take (which are actually quite small behaviors). When your belt is too tight, loosen it. When your load is too heavy, put it down. Pay yourself physically first. Allow that you take good care of yourself. Then, when you do these little things, these reachable things, these possible things for today, that gives you the ability to make your big dreams come true. If you stop for a snack when you're hungry, that's more meaningful to your body than waiting for the sumptuous meal in Paris when you retire. Take care of yourself; don't abandon yourself.

When you find there are certain situations you always come up to that you don't feel natural in, that you don't feel you are who you are in, then those are the ones to no longer deny, but to change.

The way to have what you want is to be who you are. What percentage of your day are you doing what you really want? Most people answer that less than fifteen percent of their days are how they want them to be. Ask yourself about the other eighty-five percent. It's your day. Don't you want to be a one hundred percent person?

The Abandonment Issue

If you felt abandoned as a child, chances are you've abandoned yourself. Chances are if you were abandoned, then now you don't eat right or don't have enough money to take care of yourself or in some way are personifying that feeling in your body. You are abandoning yourself.

This morning I gave an assignment to one of my students who forgets to take care of herself. I asked her to write on a yellow Post-it™:

I HAVE NEEDS

THEY ARE

_____

Then I asked her to stick it on her heart, right on her skin, and wear it all day; and every few minutes, all day long, feel it there and fill in the blank with what she needs at that moment. She just called. Her boyfriend apologized, her boss didn't slam the door, and she actually took a lunch break.

Here's a helpful wordplay: To be abundant, "U" say amen to abandonment.

You're Wonderful—Accept It

Do you have a hard time receiving love? For instance, can you accept a compliment? As much as you love them and want them, notice how you deflect compliments that come to you. Do you denigrate compliments by saying, "Oh, this old dress"; or do you deflect it if someone says "I love you"? Do you say "I love you, too,"so that you're not absorbing it, you're sending it right back like a hot potato. You're not really internalizing it and appreciating it and accepting it? See if you can stand fast—brace yourself. Be willing to receive love.

Do you know when you first said, "I'm not going to receive love because it's going to be in some way hurtful to me"? Here's how to track that back: When someone compliments you and your emotion bucket in your stomach closes down, then you can begin to see when that happened in the first place in your childhood. It can be the slightest moment, twenty-seven years ago. For instance, when you were three years old and you were wearing your special new outfit and the family was all there and they all said "Ooh, ahh, aren't you cute," and then you thought, you weren't quite sure, but there you were at three and you thought Mommy gave a disgusted look at Daddy, and you closed down instantaneously in your stomach because you realized that if you received that love from Daddy it would in some way hurt Mommy. So as loyalty to Mommy you decided not to receive that kind of compliment.

Here's a fun thing to do. Accept a compliment. How do you do that? Buy yourself a little packet of thank-you notes. You can start small, maybe get a package of twenty. Sit in your favorite place, it could be out on a park bench or curled up in your favorite chair, and send out all twenty of those cards thanking people in your life for what you have received from them this week. Thank anybody for anything.

You might think, "What have I got to thank anybody for? Nobody's complimented me or given me anything this week." Well, the point is, you have these thank-you cards, you've got to fill them out. You'll be amazed at how much has been given to you this week that you didn't realize until you had to say thank-you for it. Guaranteed, by the time you get to your twentieth card, you'll need more.

Here's an example of the extra payoff you receive once you send all the cards out. You know that you're sending them out for you so you can understand and have evidence of how much you have received. But here is the upshot. When I was going to be forty, I decided I didn't want to wimp into that age; I wanted to spring back and leap into it. My dear friend Leigh Charlton is a great photographer, and she took my quintessential forty-year-old picture, and it was really celebratory—my arms were all outstretched, hooray, hooray. So we did this photo and I glued them all on cards and sent them to everybody I knew for the first forty years of my life, thanking them for being in my life and for the contributions that they made to enhance my life. That was great fun. I enjoyed it, and that was my present to myself for forty, and that was that. But there was something else: In my travels around the country that year I saw various friends, and guess what? They all had my picture on their refrigerators with the notes that I had written! So there I was, arms outstretched in the hooray position, and I was in the daily lives of all those dear people whom I loved in the first place. So that when they would open the doors of their refrigerator, the lights would come on. What an incredible benefit!

So you see, thank you comes right back at you.

Yeah—But . . .

We've already talked about yeah-buts. It's a pretty simple concept and you got it. Notice how your yeah-buts are coming up like crazy now. This is good. This is progress. You'll be fine. Your yeah-buts will give you information about what's keeping you from following your heart.

Last week when I was doing a seminar I was talking about this idea (apparently it's a revolutionary idea, to follow your heart) and one woman said, "Yeah-but if I follow my heart, I won't have any friends." Can you see immediately what her belief said? She thought that doing what she wanted to do made her a bad person. She chose to follow her friends to do what they wanted to do. The thought never really occurred to her that she could do what she wanted to do and still be loved. I asked her if these were the friends she really wanted to have. Certainly they were because there was some benefit to her to be doing what someone else wanted to do. Maybe it was because she didn't know what she wanted to do, so she started exploring that idea last Sunday. And on Wednesday she called to tell me that she found a new friend and the reason she thinks this is a new friend is because the person asked her what she wanted to do!

I Do What I Want When I Want

What reaction does that statement arouse in you? A lot of people at my seminars will say, "If I do what I want to do when I want to do it, that will hurt other people." What makes you think that doing what you want will hurt somebody? Where did you get that belief? Where did that come from early in your life?

Guilt Is an Illusion

The belief that you can't do what you want is an illusion. You're trading off your dreams for guilt. About ninety-nine percent of guilt is self-imposed. It's not really based on anything you ever did wrong or any legitimate reason. Start today by doing something that (a) you want to do, (b) do it when you want to do it, and (c) see how that does not hurt other people. And then you can get better and bigger ideas about how you can do this. Just because you're doing what you want doesn't mean somebody else is going to be hurt by that at all. In fact, it's usually quite the opposite: Somebody else will be inspired by your freedom and join in.

Also, following your heart is holy. It leads you straight to your life purpose. There's a job you came here to do, a contribution you want to make for all of us. We want you doing what you want, because that is the world service that contributes to us all. Ask, "What is the best and highest use of my heart's desire? What is the best and highest use of the energy that I have for the day?"

As you shift your responsibilities to yourself, you won't be guilty because you'll take responsibility. Your relationships will shift and you will be heard by others and you will do what you want to do.

P.S. People will love you more.

The Answer to the Problem
That Creates Another Problem
Is Not the Answer to the Problem

There is a difference between accepting something and acknowledging that it exists. When we use the word "accepting," a lot of times we feel as if it means we have to sanction or agree with what is going on. That is simply not so. *We do not have to accept the unacceptable.* What we want to do is change how we have accepted situations from the past. We want to *acknowledge* that they existed. Then we get to say, "No, I don't accept that."

The only way to change a circumstance is to acknowledge that it is going on. One of the ways to do that is to untangle what your want is from the consequence of it. I'll give you an example. When my client Pat was little she wanted her father to stop drinking. What her mother did to solve that problem was divorce her father. Pat wanted the problem to go away; instead, her father went away. That was not the solution she wanted. So at an early age she decided to not want problems solved, because if they're solved the solution is worse. She accepted problems because she feared that the solution would be much worse than the problem was.

The answer to the problem that creates another problem is not the answer to the problem. Often we know in our heart of hearts that the solution is sometimes worse than the problem. That's why we tend to stay in the problem because we feel that we can at least accept or in some way handle it. We fear the solution and the feeling of being out of control.

Solutions to problems that are worse than the problems are fear-based. The key to finding the right solution is to go in the opposite direction—toward love. The opposite of fear is love. So when we begin to shift away from fear we always shift toward love, and in love is where the problem gets solved. All solutions that are fear-based will make the situation worse. All solutions that are love-based will make your life better because you'll no longer be living in the problem or the solution. You'll be beyond both.

Asking Directly

If you don't ask for what you want, you won't get what you want. Confusion about this usually starts very early in our lives when we ask for something. When we don't get it, we think, "I'd better not ask for it. I'd better find other ways to come up with this thing." An example from my life: When I was about six years old we had a small fire in the kitchen and the kitchen smelled yucky, and I said, "I don't want to eat in the kitchen. I want to eat on the porch." So I got to eat on the porch. I was sitting out there all by myself, and I still remember where I was sitting on the porch. I was sitting on the floor directly in front of the door, facing the door, clearly anxious to have my family come out and eat on the porch, too. But there I was by myself. I got what I asked for. I asked to eat on the porch, but that's not what I wanted. What I really wanted was for the whole family to eat out there together, and I did not ask directly for what I wanted.

Look at your childhood and find the experience when you asked for something and got what it was you asked for, and it wasn't what you wanted. What scene from your childhood pops into your head? I formed a belief while I was sitting there on the porch, sitting facing the door, that if I asked for what I wanted then I was going to get it and it was going to be yucky, so I guess I better not ask for what I want. Find your experience and discover what belief you made. Write that down, write down the experience and then write down the belief you formed, and then change the belief you formed to a new belief. You can ask directly for what you want, and by asking directly for what you want you get it; you get it from others and you get it from yourself because you're clear about what it is you want. If you can ask people clearly and directly, "Can you do this for me," "Can you help me in some way to get this for myself," then they can respond to you right away. They can say no or yes and you're off and running with no subterfuge involved. It's honest. It's powerful. It works.

Once you see the power in asking directly, wisdom sets in. You understand that the success in getting your answer is in how you ask the question.

What You Want When You Want It All

Is this you: "I Can't Get Enough; Give Me Everything"?

The answer to getting it all is to appreciate what you have. At Christmas I was with two kids. One opened his gifts one at a time and was rhapsodic about all the gifts and the paper, too; the other kid tore through every one of the presents, finished quickly, and complained, "I want more."

Learn appreciation. Be willing to take lovingly each small gift of life and receive it and acknowledge that you have received it, and appreciate it and allow it in. You won't be happy with more until you're happy with what you've got.

Tune in your receiver so that you can get all the stations clearly and all the entertainment value and all the joys and the richness coming in at you. Use all your senses. It's all going on, but if you don't turn on your set, how are you going to experience it?

Are You a Bottomless Bucket?

Were you deprived? You can't help feeling that your needs never are satisfied. It's okay.

Here's how you got that way. When you were a kid, nothing satisfied the need. The need had nothing to do with things gotten from the outside, so when you did get things from the outside it felt like not enough because it didn't fill the need. It didn't stop the emptiness.

Here's late-breaking news. Your neediness has nothing to do with your current needs. You're an adult, you can satisfy your current needs as they come up. Satisfy them, take care of yourself. Say this: "I can satisfy all of my current needs. I take good care of myself." Meanwhile, work to uncover what past needs didn't get met. As you uncover them, you can decide how to satisfy them. Teddy bears are a big adult business.

Here's a today exercise to satisfy a yesterday need. Maybe you uncovered that you got needy around asking for help. You asked for help as a kid and didn't get it, so as an adult you don't dare ask anything of anyone. Change that today. Go out to lunch with friends and say, "Please pass the salt."

Start small. Build.

Now you may say, "What do you mean, I can satisfy my current need? My current need is to buy the Pan Am Building!" That is not your current need. Your need is to buy the Pan Am Building so that your father will be proud of you. Save twelve billion dollars. Be proud of yourself.

Some wants are ungotten because we think somebody else has to give us love, respect, approval. . . . Go directly to those qualities within. How would it feel inside if you had your parents' approval? What does that do to your posture, your breathing, your ideas you can act on tomorrow? Give that to yourself. Fill your needs from within.

The Only Job for You

You are your job. If you are doing your you job right, you can work in the buzzsaw department at Sears and you're doing your job because *you* are your job. If you are in the buzzsaw department at Sears and you can't do the you job, then get out of the buzzsaw department at Sears.

By the way, I'm not suggesting that you then become chairman of the board someplace. You don't have to have a la-de-da job; you can have a forty-hour factory week. You can do that. That is a choice of supporting yourself and having life go on beyond the job. That's perfectly fine if you can do that. If that doesn't work or you aren't in harmony while you're at the job, then that's not the job for you. Part of your job is to find the job that is your job. If you're giving forty or more of your hours to something other than you, that is not a good use of forty of your precious hours.

What Is Noble Work?

You. You are noble work. So whatever your heart desires is the work that is noble for you. Nobility is rampant. It is everywhere, in the joy of your job. I love the nobility of some waitresses. Just when you begin to form the thought that you want more butter, they whisk it right over to your table. That's impeccability! Make your job your world service; make it your contribution.

Bo Diddley did an ad for a pawn shop and a disc jockey was very critical about it, saying how dare he do a pawn shop ad; it was beneath him. And Bo said, "Make the money you need to make to continue to do what you do." Very cool. If you are above it all or if it's immoral, don't take the job. If the corporation you've applied to is killing off the swamp-life behind the town, don't take the job. If you don't care about the swamplife behind the town, take the job, enjoy yourself. Follow your heart where it leads. That's what you get your paycheck for.

P.S. For those who consider themselves human and then some. . . .

The God Job

Attention, gods who have come to earth to do a God job. Are you having a hard time being human? Here's the key. Being human is the answer to getting your God job done. You fear that if you become human you will forget your God job, but here is the key: The way to do the God job is to be human and the God job gets done.

If you feel that your job is to uplift the human race, put on a tie, get a car, drive to a stoplight, look at the driver next to you. When the driver looks at you—smile. Pull away. You've done your God job.

▪ *Allow Money*

Is Money Really the Bottom Line?

Along about now you might be saying, "Pooey, if I had the money I wouldn't have to deal with all of this. I wouldn't have to look at what I deny; I wouldn't have to have this headache. I could just go buy what makes me happy." Well, here's the deal about money: Money issues are never about money. They are always about love.

Whatever lack you felt in your life as a child, look now in your adult life and see how that lack personifies itself in your money.

Our Lady of Perpetual Debt

Do you worship at the altar of overspending? Are you in debt? In trouble with the IRS? Up to your limit on credit cards? Unable to face Uncle Bob because you owe him for the Naugahyde recliner chair?

A great deal of debt is our way of collecting punitive damages. If you think the world owes you a living, your debt is equal to what you think you are owed. You want to find a way to collect for all your suffering. Once you spend up to your credit limit and that doesn't satisfy you, then the debt will feel the same as the original problem felt.

The Bankrupt Heart

Whatever your past relationship with love, see how it has created your present relationship with money. If you have trouble with the IRS, look to the turmoil you have internally. If you always had drama around money because your family was broke when you were a child, you can be very, very wealthy now but still have the equal drama around money.

There's Finally Interest in You

Credit card abuse is most especially amassed by people in their thirties. That is when you have an issue around who takes care of you. Credit cards become your substitute provider if you've weaned off being taken care of by your parents and cannot and don't want to take care of yourself. Just because you walk out of the store with your package and you didn't pay for it doesn't mean it's free. It doesn't mean someone else bought it for you. You bought it and you owe 19.8 percent more than the purchase price.

If you are in debt, you have an underlying grasp on what it means to experience credit. Somebody extended something to you (love, attention, faith in you, belief that you were good for it). Pay off the debt; experience having credit. Turn it around. Get it off your back and to your advantage. Have your credit work for you, not against you.

How?

Do you feel as if there's nothing you can do? You'll never get out? You'll never be free? You've tried everything and it's not enough, it's never enough? Do you do this: You can't pay all the bills, so you don't pay any?

Here is a most elegant idea to introduce to yourself: The little thing makes the big difference. Always go from where you are, what you can do. You think it's small. *Do it. Do it.* Do the very small thing.

Know, please know, the mightiness of the small step.

The High Cost of Being Broke

Having money always changes your mind about the fantasy you had around money. If you are broke you might lust after the top restaurant. When you have money, the good little old tasty place is exactly where you want to eat.

How to Be a This-Minute Millionaire

If you find yourself longing for the 3.2-million-dollar mansion, see how much pocket money you're carrying. The less money in your pocket, the bigger the money fantasy.

Raise the amount of your pocket money. If you usually carry about three dollars, up it to twenty. Give yourself a chance at spontaneous spending. Be able to afford two scoops of Hagen Daz ice cream just because you feel like it. That's rich. Practice being a millionaire-by-the-minute. You will see that it actually costs you less than depriving yourself and stretching for the big items. Deprivation makes you want more and bigger; satisfaction makes you satisfied.

Open your avenues of revenue. Practice having what you have. Rather than reach out, reach in. Experience abundance in what you have. Open to the abundance that is already yours. More will come. Honest.

Money Is Not Security

If you are spending money you don't have for things you don't need, you are probably using money as emotional support rather than financial support. You can have stocks and bonds and insurance and mutual funds and your Aunt Betty's mattress stuffed with ten-dollar bills. You may have all this for security. But see where the security is . . . it's in your thinking. "I'll have $128,473.82 and then I'll feel secure." It's not the amount. It's the thought. If you are amassing a fortune so that you can feel completely secure, here's news. There is never enough to be impervious to insecurity. Protection by isolation doesn't work; you can always be attacked at your fear. Do this instead: Declare yourself safe at any bank account.

How Much Is Priceless?

Do you know how much it costs to buy a million-dollar feeling? You can't buy it—for any price. However, you can give it to yourself free, any time. When do you want to start?

Rich Within

So again, money issues are never about money. They are always about love. If you want to change your money issues, then begin to start clearing the place where you first experienced a bankrupt heart. If you are broke, you are broke for very good reasons. Identify why you struggle with money. What unfinished business do you have about love? Take care of it.

Follow your love. Where do you stop love to make money? Where do you think you can't be loved until you're rich? Open your love bank; be willing to be loved.

Get your pay. Be free to be rich!

Just Give Me the Cash

Now you may say, "Fine, good, all well and true. But how do I pay my rent today?" Well, I'll tell you. Look at how you have struggled and paid your rent in the past. Look at how you have grappled to find it before. This is not the first time you couldn't pay your rent. The other times you worked it out. What way did you work it out? Now, you may say "Yeah-but, those were not satisfactory ways. I want a better way. I want the money in my hand right now." All right, look at how you were successful before. You always came up with it. How did you do that?

Money Is Communication

The value of being broke and being in jeopardy about money requires you to reach out. You've got to ask somebody for a job, for a loan, for a place to sleep on a couch. So, if you are in money jeopardy, it causes you to communicate with other people, which is perfect, because money is communication. Money comes through other people. In the U.S. our money is stamped "In God We Trust." If you trust God, you won't be afraid to talk to people to get the money God gave them to hold for you. So if it comes from other people, you have to communicate with them. And if you're not communicating with them, then guess what— your money quotient goes down.

Here's how it works: If you're broke and you can't stand that you're broke and it forces you to call your brother whom you haven't talked to in six years for the money, this is communication. It's a good use of why you're broke. You're so desperate that you have to talk to him even though you can't stand to talk to him. The money issue is the thing that causes you to communicate with your estranged brother. Now, you ask him for the money, he'll probably say no, but he might say yes. The point is, you've communicated, you've broken through. The communication, the connection is the jackpot. Getting a job is communicating. Quitting a job is communicating. Even getting in the car to go to the job makes you a *commuter.* The closer you address your honest needs, the more likely money will flow. In other words, the clearer your communication, the higher the paycheck.

The Art of Forward Financing

You say again, "Great, fine, all well and good. But how do I make my rent *today*?" Two things are going on simultaneously. There's this month's rent you need to pay and there's the future months' rent you will need to pay. You're going to be satisfying both needs simultaneously. When you are working to pay the rent today, you're also working to pay future rent so that you're not going to be in this position anymore. It's very frustrating to need $100 today. If someone offers you a job that pays $100 by next Tuesday and you're not going to want to take that job because it doesn't satisfy the $100 dilemma you've got today—take the job. What it does do is solve next week's $100 dilemma.

What you're doing is you're getting out and you're being out ever after, and that requires two kinds of tools. You're not going to "get out" until you also fix "being out" at the same time. Simultaneously, you are working with solving the immediate problem (rent for this month) and the once-and-for-allness of having the future rents. See that the one does not frustrate the other and cancel each other out. So, if you need $100 today and the offer is $100 for next week, take it. You've solved next week. When you solve next week, that leads to solving this week. It's not the other way around. Heal the present by taking action in the future.

Think of it this way: Now you're solvent for next week. A person who is solvent for next week has a much better chance of being solvent this week. You can do it; you can actually come up with $100 for next week, so that gives you the confidence then to come up with $100 for this week.

Scared About the Money

Is your bank account half full or half empty? Money is pretty much an illusion. Once we give up worrying about money, a miracle happens: There is money enough.

It's curious because the amount you worry about money is the exact amount of money you don't have. As the worry quotient goes down, the money quotient goes up. Try it. Time spent worrying does not generate money. Once you stop the worrying, it gives you time to take actions that bring money in. Every time you find yourself obsessing over money see it as a thought, and a thought is changeable, so then your work is to change the thought, and once you change the thought you'll see how the money will be enough. It will come in for you. You won't starve. You'll be okay.

Money tension is created when you look at how much you want and don't have. Instead look at how much you do have this minute. When you look at something as is, you let go of neediness; you let go of a sense of lacking. If you only look at the result you want, all you see is what you don't have, what you don't like, all the neediness that isn't yet satisfied. Observe without judgment. Just say to yourself, "It's what it is." Then you will begin to get more. When you look at how it is and feel how you want to feel, you can have your heart's desire. You're experiencing the feeling already. That's Feelization. Feel it. Have it.

Beyond Money

Are you living on credit cards and praying for a condo, a soul mate, straight teeth? Are you wondering when you'll get yours? You may be asking yourself, "If I'm so spiritually correct, why can't I pay my light bill?" You *can* have it all . . . you believe that; and yet where is your Ferrari?

My theory is that you are a forerunner for the new economy. You wanted it all and actually you now have it, but it feels like too much to do with not enough time to do it. And you asked for a million dollars and you still can't pay the rent.

You question the methods. You question your techniques. You are demanding that you get yours and you haven't gotten yours. Look again. See with new eyes. See what you have and know you created it—if you want it in a different form, use Feelization to allow precision to get you your dream. Feel, with precision, the feeling you want to have when you get what you want to have. Continue to perfect that feeling to have it feel completely good and feel completely how you want it. The effort is in the impeccability of your precision.

Abundance is an acquired taste. It's not excess; it's deep richness. It's the experience of more things and people and feelings connecting, not separating. It's all the pieces of your puzzle becoming connected to the bigger picture.

If you want the penthouse so that you don't have to have neighbors, that wish will not feel abundant when you get it. Abundance is when you are *a part of* rather than *apart from* others. Wishes that separate will keep you in lack; wishes that include more life will expand your abundance.

We are moving from an addictive society, where more looks like something that comes from the outside, to a partnership society, where abundance emerges from the inside.

We are coming out of a time of wanting on an external level. The external symbols of abundance are changing. It used to be that a limo meant rich. Now limos are for teens on prom night. Abundance has become larger. We are wishing for abundance and getting the new wave of what abundance really is, but we are still watching for it to come in the old way, in the form of status and better than others. When we are willing to feel what it really feels like, we will experience the new abundance, which is connection.

People are attending twelve-step programs in droves. They are experiencing fellowship. It's a new way to socialize. It used to be that people had meaningful experiences in hotel rooms. They still do, but it's in the meeting rooms with three hundred other seminar attendees. When we can hug a hundred strangers on Saturday, maybe on Monday we can talk to our kids and they'll actually take out the garbage.

A sense of community is forming now to create a family for the twenty-first century, where people can tell the truth about themselves and what they want and need and how they can be loved. We are moving into that time of community—away from dependence and independence and toward interdependence, from "You've got the money; you take care of me" or "I've got the money; I don't need you" to "I can contribute this skill. Thanks for giving me that help." Our relationship to money is moving from fear to love. We are more important than money.

Enough Is Enough

This is an enough is enough break. Put your hand over your heart and say, "I am enough." When you say that and you're satisfied, then go out and play right now. If not, then go out and play anyway, and take this symbol with you.

Every time you think you're too tall, too old, too dumb, too too too—it's not so. You're just right.

▪ *Above Fear*

Be Unafraid to Be Afraid

I just did some work with students who, very recently, graduated from college. The main subject of our talks was "So now what?" I noticed something major. The ones who came from high-end economic backgrounds were scared and wanted to fall back into their comfort zones. Those who came from working class backgrounds were also scared, but their fear moved them *toward* their comfort zones.

Where is your comfort zone, behind you or ahead of you? Use your fear in your favor. Be comforted while you take the giant step.

One concept I worked on with the graduates was this: Of course you're scared. It's okay to be scared. Just because you're scared doesn't mean you have to stop. You can be scared and go.

Here's what I did during my dealmaking days in Hollywood. I had an electric blanket on my bed. All day I kept it turned to a high number. I knew that any time it got cold in the world I could come home and pull the warm blanket over my head.

What small sweet thing can you do for yourself? Pick out something now. Give yourself some tender care, then hit the street, kiddo.

You Are the World

Say, for instance, as a baby you were left alone overlong in your crib. You were hungry, cold, and crying. No one came. Imagine your overwhelming helplessness. How could you do anything about that as a baby? What you did was you got constraints in your body. You got the fear in your neck, the cold in your shoulders, the hunger in the pit of your stomach. In fact, the only action you could take was to feel the enormity of the outside circumstance *inside your body.* The overwhelming circumstance was then lodged in your body. Thirty years later you feel hunger in the pit of your stomach and you connect it to that original situation. The good news is that now you can do something about the hunger in your stomach. You can eat or you can stop overeating. You can free yourself of protecting yourself from taking care of what didn't get taken care of and take care of yourself today.

We can heal those overwhelming outside circumstances from within. Because that's where the slings and arrows penetrated. Those are the wounds to be healed; the slings and arrows are long gone. When history repeats itself, it's because we haven't healed those original wounds in our bodies yet.

We are human beings. We have bodies. In our bodies is where we heal ourselves.

Obstacles Are Only There
in Case You Care to Stop

Let's do another Feelization exercise, knowing what you
know now and how you've identified some of the obstacles
that have been standing between you and what you want.
I invented this exercise for one of my USC students who
was pining all semester over his dream girl. In six weeks
he still hadn't even spoken to her. I drew a horizontal line
on the blackboard and put an X at the right hand end of
the line.

————————————————————————————————— X

I gave him the chalk and asked that if the X is the result
he wants—having a date with the dream girl—then where
is he along the line? He put a tiny X as far over to the left
as possible. So then I asked him to put as many Xs as he
thought it would take to get from where he was to his dream
date. You can do that now. Think of the right hand of the
line as the life you want to have, and put an X along the line
where you think you are on the way to getting that life.

Now, put Xs along the line to see how many Xs it takes
to get from where you are now to the result. Since you read
the section "Why You Don't Think That you Get What You
Want," you are noticing familiar obstacles you have seen
in your path in recent times and can start identifying some
of those Xs.

What does each X stand for? For instance, you have to
lose fifty-two pounds. You don't really want the dream girl;
you want to have the girl as a dream so that you don't have
to go out on a date with anybody real. Identify what each
X represents for you. Now you can see clearly the steps
from where you are to your result.

If we were going to do a Goal Plan, we'd schedule this out. But we're not going to do that. We're going to use Feelization. This is not a Five-Year Plan. This is this minute. So now feel the feeling that you want, in essence, when you get your Big X, your dream date, whatever it is. Feel what that feels like now, in your body. Then go back and feel what the other X felt like, the beginning X. Now notice the differences. Go down your list of all the other Xs you identified and see how each feels. See if the feeling you have graduates from the beginning X to the end X. Do the Xs in between get you from the beginning X to the end X?

Notice the feelings in your body. They are very subtle; you don't have to hurt yourself. Notice if you clear your throat—there's some anger going on. Look at one of the Xs that has to do with an obstacle around anger. Notice if you begin to start breathing funny. Your heart might like to open wider.

When you read "Why You Don't Think That You Get What You Want," did you get some aha's? Start to see how they give you information about where the blocks are now with your Xs.

This is a simple little thing—just X your way into existence. Go ahead and do it. It works!

Are You Living on Empty?

Do this exercise: Think of ten things that are low-ebb annoyances in your life, the small areas that are limited or lacking. Examples:

> Your front door lock is loose and you have to jiggle it to get the door open every time.

> There's a pretty much empty jar of jelly in the refrigerator, not enough to put on a sandwich, but too much to throw out.

> The batteries are dead in the emergency flashlight.

> You always run out of toilet paper.

Now do this: Master the small corner. (I think this is a Zen phrase.) Master abundance in jelly. Buy a new jar. Master abundance in opening doors. Get out your screwdriver and fix your doorknob.

Eliminate the low-ebb annoyances from your life. When you do, your body will relax and open in places you didn't even know you had. Release where you carry abandonment. Always give your body the best choices. You are the world.

How to Feel Feelings

Pick a feeling you've experienced recently, preferably a feeling you don't like to feel. There are two things to talk about here. One, you're feeling a feeling. Two, your thought is that you don't like the feeling.

Now, here's what you're going to do. *Detach* the thought from the feeling. (Note: We're going to be very heads-up about not denying the feeling.) When you're feeling a feeling, feel it. What you're after is this: Feel the feeling; change the thought.

What are some things you have done about this feeling in the past? Have you tried to run from it and then noticed a thousand pound knapsack on your back in your freedom run? Have you sat with it? Felt the feeling? Great. However, you might have noticed that this is not easy. Most of us as adults are just beginning to learn how to feel our feelings after a lifetime of knowing how not to feel.

There is help! The secret is this: Feel how you feel and not judge how you feel or deny how you feel or try to change how you feel. The secret is to *value* how you feel.

Our feelings like it when we don't require them to be different from what they actually are. Do you notice that when you're in a circumstance you don't like, it bothers you at some moments and not at other moments? That's because the circumstance is not what you're bothered by. You're bothered by the thought. Usually you can find the thought in your body. Find that the thought is floating around in your body. You may pace, you may wring your hands, your throat may tighten. What happens in your body when you are thinking the thought?

When you are aware of the changes in your body when something is on your mind, then you are aware of how you are experiencing your thoughts in your body. It's an actual, tangible way of seeing how your thoughts work in you.

The thought finds a way to amplify itself by attaching to some aspect of your body. For instance, if you are feeling empty, if that is an overriding feeling that is your disposition, then chances are you are either quite overweight and can't seem to ever fill that emptiness or, as with one of my clients who is very, very thin, you complain of the enormous emptiness that you feel within. Your thought attaches itself onto a part of your physiology. It's amazing what you can do, very simply, within your physiology to acknowledge the thought in there. Know it is within your power to integrate it.

Your emotional body is wrapped in your physical body. When you find there is a huge thing outside yourself that is overwhelming, the feeling that you're having about it is not outside yourself. The feeling that you're having is in your body.

I'll give you a really simple example from my life: I was fogged in at JFK airport. There were more people per square inch than there were square inches. This called for floating on the circumstance. As you know, it's easy to be enlightened on a mountaintop. But how do you do it when eight hundred people are fighting over the last four hot dogs? I was sitting on the floor on my bags in front of a fellow who was reading, perfectly happy in the chaos. I was getting more and more furious at him because he was what I wanted to be. He was completely comfortable in himself. The main thing that bothered me was that he was swinging his naked foot in my face. Every time it swung up it got funnier looking and more grotesque, until this perfectly wonderful person, who had the answer to life in JFK airport, was an object of my murderous thoughts. I wanted to strangle him. And then it dawned on me what this foot was doing in my face. It was a messenger foot. I realized that my feet were really, really cold, and when I realized this I got out my Mickey Mouse socks and put them on and I was, within moments, deeply rhapsodic.

So here is the point: I found my emotion in my body. When I was able to take care of that very small body detail, the rest of me was able to follow that.

So if you change one small thing, the small change spontaneously changes the circumstance. Very powerful stuff. Put your socks on—the world changes.

The Difference Between Observation and Judgment

I use the phrase "begin to notice" a lot throughout the book. Have you noticed? The reason is this: For the changes that you are now making in your reality, you are shifting from judging your circumstances to observing them. In judgment you look at what you think is going on and don't like it. For instance, you are happy and quiet and suddenly a neighbor turns on talk radio so loud it vibrates your fillings. You hate this and want to kill your neighbor. But what is really going on in you? Notice how your body was in repose and then what changes occurred when the loud noise started. Where in your body did you feel it? Notice your thoughts. How did you go from repose to plans of murder? What thoughts were in between? How many thoughts? How intense were they? Did you think of a time when you were three and with your mother? Did you think of your boss and an incident at work last week? What action do you immediately take? If you don't take any action, how do you feel about that?

The point is this: When you go from judgment in a situation ("My neighbor is a two-headed brain-dead no-goodnik") to "Isn't this interesting that I have an immediate headache?" you can begin to find *how thoughts form*. Is this a new thought coming from a high light plane above your head, or is this a thought dredged up from a cesspool of familiar thoughts you've had before? Observe that the neighbor's radio noise may be brand new, but the thoughts that it triggers seem to be attached to a whole string of thoughts you've had before.

Okay, you say "I observe this; I see how my thoughts form and I formed them in this same pattern a million times before. Same old, same old. So now what?" Just observe.

You're not out to change it here because that would mean you were judging it and requiring it to change. Just observe. As you observe, it changes spontaneously.

"Fine. It changes spontaneously, but meanwhile my neighbor with his talking radio is still a two-headed no-goodnik." Continue to observe. You're angry. Find it in your body. Who were you originally angry at? Who was the very first two-headed no-goodnik you encountered in your life?

Observe, and find it. Have you been carrying fear in your stomach since you were age three? Observe, and in the observation you'll release where it was lodged in your body. And in the release, change will then occur spontaneously. The original experience is no longer attached to the new experience. Suddenly the radio doesn't matter or you get the idea to ask your neighbor to turn it down.

Exercise: Pick a ten-minute time to yourself, maybe during a morning shower or driving. Observe your random thoughts. How many are thoughts you've never had before? Go ahead, be amazed at how many times you think the same old thought and it wasn't a fun thought the first zegamillion times you thought it. Are you willing to think some brand new shine thoughts? Feel a shift. Now you're ready for an only-new-thoughts-allowed conversation with a loved one. Try it for five minutes. Expand to a whole evening. See how this totally familiar person becomes a fascinating new resource in your life. Welcome to your new probable reality.

The Danger of Affirmations

If we drum into our heads a new belief before it is ready to be believed, we pour shellac over our old fears. Now our fears that were buried in the first place are imbedded in yet another layer of goo. We can certainly work to change beliefs, but we might want to take a look at why they are there in the first place and what benefits we are getting from them. If we accept our yucky-part-old-belief, it's going to be a lot easier to live with and say good-bye to than if we hatefully try to push it out the door.

I'll tell you an old pattern I changed so that you'll get the idea. When I was eight, we lived in the projects on the south side of Chicago. I saw that there was no money and, as a way to survive, decided "don't need money." Children make survival decisions according to the skills they have at the time. What decisions did you make that are lasting your whole lifetime?

Those decisions, made so early, were very sound and saved your life. At age eight I created an ingenious set of survival techniques to get through life with no money. Later, however, I didn't need to get by on no money. I was an adult and could find a better solution, like, for instance, make money. So I set about changing my belief.

If I affirmed my way out of "don't need money" before I honored why I set that belief in the first place, I would not value that I had been ingenious and would not understand why I had decided what I did. If all you cure is symptoms, the next ones will be doozies.

Watch your symptoms because your symptoms are there to give you information and to help you. They are a clue to the real emotion that is much, much bigger underneath.

Look at where your heart is bankrupt. Start cultivating love paychecks.

Tsk Taken to Task

If you find yourself saying things like, "Oh, what a shame" and "tsk," look again. Look at the benefit of why you think it's a shame. What is the value in feeling that the atrocity that's happening to you is an atrocity? See where the suffering has a use for you and something that you can learn from. This covers big categories, too, such as disease and death and extreme suffering. When you look and you suffer over it, there's a loss that you're not yet willing to have, because you feel that if you lose it you will have less. And loss is always to open up to more.

Why You Are Confused

Do you find you are at a time in your life when you don't know what to do next? Hooray and congratulations! What you are in is a transition. Did you ever see a bird float on an air draft and every now and then flutter its wings to stay on course? When we are in transition we are in a whole lot of wing fluttering. You may think you don't know where you're going. You know profoundly the feeling of batting your wings about. You want to be on course and the way you think you'd be on course is to see your destination ahead of you. This is the exact reason you're confused. Trying to make sense of where you're going is confusing because you can't know where you're going until you get there. Yes, it can be frightening to keep stepping one step and the next step and the next step. But that's all any of us has. Anything else is an illusion. You want to see where you're going so you know where to go. No wonder you're confused.

Try this: Let go of having your mind work over and over about "Is it this way, is it this way, is it this way?" and work on trust. Work on the *feeling* of willingness to go forward into the void, willing to know that your path is already set and you know full well how you're proceeding. It's just that it feels uncomfortable and questionable at the time because your eye is looking where you're going rather than trusting you to go. Hold to the feeling of what you want. The feeling will then guide you to your heart's desire. Feel it in your heart. Have it in your life.

Outcome Is an Inside Job

I was walking along the beach. There were four boogie board boys enjoying the surf, and before they noticed me coming they were experts at the waves. Never a splash or a fall. Then they saw me coming. Oh my gosh, maybe I was a chick or a fox or a possibility! They immediately became self-conscious and terrible. They were falling into the surf and smacking into the sand. But as I got closer they could see that I'm old enough to be a chick or a fox for their fathers. So they relaxed and they were experts again.

Thus I correlate . . . a self-conscious boogie boarder wipes out. If we are attached to outcome, if we try to get a particular result, if we insist upon riding the waves in a cool manner and not making mistakes, then we wipe out. But if we do it from the inside out, just because it feels good on the inside, the outcome doesn't matter a bit. And guess what? That's when the outcome is great and magical.

Why Overachievers Feel Like Failures

Here's my theory regarding overachieving. There's something you wanted early in your life, something fundamental, like Dad's love or Mom's good health. But no matter what you achieve in your life, you feel you failed at getting that primary want.

Fill in this blank:

"When I was a kid, I wanted more than anything to

_____ .

As an adult, I'm still using my energy to

_____ ."

Do you notice how you keep doing more and more and it feels like less? It *is* less. Whatever you achieve, you feel deep down that you failed at the real thing you were doing it for.

Lots of rock stars achieve tremendous fame and fortune when all they really wanted was to get Daddy's attention. They may still not achieve getting Daddy's attention. Another gold record is not going to do it.

Here's what to do to release yourself from trying harder and doing more and still not feeling good enough. Go to the mirror, look yourself in the eye, and say, "My primary want was _____ . *I failed.*" Really feel this now. "I failed." Allow the clump of feelings to well up through your emotion bucket (stomach) and up through your throat (the lifetime prison of all the feelings you didn't shout out or talk through). Allow this feeling of failure to get out and be gone. Because here's what comes after it: A tremendous feeling of self-love that you *did* achieve what you wanted. You got your heart's desire from you.

At age three I set out to cure alcoholism in my father. My plan was, "I'll cure him; then he'll get up off the floor and take care of me." I didn't cure him of alcoholism. I failed. It took until I was an adult to forgive myself for not curing alcoholism at age three. Once I faced my primary failure, I saw that I *did* get what I wanted. My Dad did take care of me because I learned from his absence to take care of myself. That's what I achieved. My father was a great provider.

Now Let's Do Recess.

This is for high achievers. Everybody else can go take a nap. (It would be great for the achievers to take a nap too, but you won't. You know how you are. So this is for you.)

I'm calling this the Do-Nothing Exercise for Over-achievers because if you're an overachiever you understand "do." You might not yet thoroughly understand "be." Since you probably love goals, the goal for this is to do nothing until you experience being.

Here's how: Sit on a couch. Period. That's it. Just sit. No TV, no crossword puzzle. Sit. Can you do it for ten minutes? See.

What do you notice? What thoughts come up? How does it feel in your body? Is your body racing to catch up to something while you're forcing it to stop? Is your body more tired than you thought you were? Are you screaming to get up and go do? Just notice.

One of the values of this exercise is that it gives you tremendous information about what keeps you overachieving. The thoughts that surface will start to form a theme. Maybe you've been keeping yourself busy to hold down a whole reservoir of tears. When you're sitting on the couch, you'll begin to start feeling the floodgates. Maybe you want to hurry and finish your ten minutes before your father finds out you're doing nothing.

Here's an example of when I invented this: Often, Christmas is the season to be inundated. So for some years my policy has been "do less, enjoy more." Last year I found I was going faster than myself and thought, "What is this?" So I sat on the couch and watched my thoughts form. I discovered that everything I wanted to get up and go do was to fix something. I couldn't think of anything beyond an activity of fixing, so then I asked, "Who am I if I'm not fixing?" And a great freedom came over me. There's more to life than fixing, so when I stopped fixing there was room that day for the more-to-life part to fill in.

If your idea of yourself is that you have to fix things and people, then things and people will continue to break so you have a job to do. When you quit the job, there's no need for the job to exist because the job existed for *you.*

Pretty soon with this couch-sitting exercise you will get so good at it that you might want to graduate to the floor. Just lie down on the floor and let the floor hold you. Let your monkey mind drain out through your back and into the floor. This is actually an official yoga position. It's called "The Dead Man's Pose." So being goal-oriented, as you are, you have something to look forward to.

The Difference Between Old Patterns You Don't Want and Throwing the Baby Out with the Bath Water

There are some patterns that are fine. They belong to you. They are you. You want them. It's okay to be that way. I have a friend who's very busy. His house is Grand Central. Every now and then he will rent a sleeping apartment just to get away from all the activities at home to go and just be quiet. Each time he starts out with the bed and quiet and nothing to work on. And pretty soon the new apartment looks like the last one, and the one before that. And there are certain things he needs and brings in and it becomes his place, like all the other ones before. This is fine; this is him. These things are the basics that suit him.

Notice how you re-create the same again and again, like, for instance, the second junk drawer in your kitchen. It's not that one junk drawer has the scissors and the screwdriver and the other junk drawer has the coupons and the Scotch Tape. It's that they both have the same hodge-podge. Forgive yourself for being who you are and the natural state of how you re-create yourself again and again.

I Can't Take It Anymore

Good. Don't.

No Such Thing as Too Much Fun

When my client Jerry would play, as a child, he would be having a great time, losing himself in joy when his mother would yell at him: "Stop that!" He said that his whole body would shut down. As an adult, when he notices he's having fun he shuts down.

Since Jerry's father was an alcoholic, one of the reasons his mother curtailed Jerry's fun was her way of dealing with excess. She wanted to control and limit excess so it wouldn't get out of hand.

Once we identified this, Jerry looked at his life in a whole new way. He used to splurge with lavish credit card abuse and then go cold turkey on deprivation and self-punishment. He never enjoyed either extreme. The middle wasn't a place he could live, because when his mother insisted upon that for him, it felt, in his body, like death. He used to say, "I'll die before I'll be middle class," and so he'd always been broke or rich, never even. Now he's exploring the middle ground: the wealth of possibilities between no watch and a Rolex. And he's having fun!

What keeps you from having all the fun you want to have? Can you enjoy yourself? Can you let yourself have it?

How to Use Your Skills on Yourself

We're used to processing failure. "Why didn't it work?"; "How can I get out of this?"; "What am I doing wrong?"; "What is everybody else doing wrong?"; "It's his fault."; "It's her fault." Processing failure keeps you failing. What you want to do is observe and process your success. See what did work, see how you are good at certain things, and then use those skills in areas of your life that you want to work on. For example, say you're really good with food intake and ho hum with money. Recognize your good skills and cross them over to other areas of your life. I had a client who was always struggling with money. Also she was really slim and healthy. We worked on how she was failing at money by working on how she was successfully slim.

I asked my client to make a list of about one hundred skills she had in the food intake department. Then she factored those into how she works with her money: bringing it in, spending it, and saving it.

I asked her questions about how she knew to budget her sugar intake so that she always stayed about the same weight. She told me, "If I see that I start gaining a couple of pounds, then I taper off." So we crossed that skill over to money. When she saw that she was overspending, she could taper off. She said, "I watch what I eat. I always want to give myself what my body needs. If I have a chili dog one day then I'm going to make sure I have vegetables the next day." That statement gave us information about how she related to money. Is overspending having to do with "giving yourself what your body needs"? We found that each time she overspent at the mall she was hungry. Since she was very good at satisfying the need in herself when she was hungry, at the mall she satisfied her "hunger" by buying shoes. When she recognized this, she didn't need to give herself shoes—she would give herself a sandwich. (Conversely, if you are overweight and go to the mall for a sandwich, put it down and buy shoes.)

If you are spending on nonessentials, can you balance that with providing for your necessities? Instead of the $700 alligator belt, can you get really excited about groceries? (If you were deprived as a kid, chances are you feel a need for external stuff to satisfy that early internal deprivation.) The best way to balance that now is to provide for your neediness with small indulgences while providing for your needs. Buy a greeting card and send it to yourself; also, pay the light bill.

This exercise will show you how factoring skills can work in your life. At the top of one side of your paper write, "I am really good at _____ . Fill in the skill that you're really good at, and then write "I would like to use my _____ skills in _____ ." Put in the category that you'd like to work better. Now, make a list of your specific success skills—you're a good listener, you pace yourself well, you don't smack your lips when you chew, anything that you're good at in your good area. On the other side of the paper cross over and see how you can use each skill in the other category of your life. This works because you get to use skills you already have. There's nothing new you have to learn. You're familiar with these skills. You can easily use your successful skills in other areas of your life.

The other benefit of this exercise is that you begin to see how you are creating, on purpose, your difficulty in the food category or the money category or whatever category, because you'll see that you already have the skills built in to eliminate the problem. Then you can ask yourself, "Why am I not using these skills?" And then the motivations and the real reasons behind the thing will begin to start showing themselves. *Bon appétit.*

How to Expand Time

Are you pressed for time? Is there not enough time? Let's expand time. Try this: The next time you are rushing with no time to spare, when you can't possibly go faster, the next time that happens, s l o w d o w n. Expand time. You will be amazed how well it works.

Being on Time

For some people it is physically impossible to be on time. You know who they are. They just can't do it. It's practically a genetic disorder. Here is a major rule of nature: When you leave for a destination after the time you're supposed to arrive at the destination, then you won't get there on time. If you're supposed to be downtown at 6 o'clock and it's 6 o'clock now, you're late.

Of all the people who suffer from chronic lateness, 80 percent just need a simple lesson in the art of backtiming. If your destination is twenty minutes away and you have to be there in twenty minutes, leave now.

If you know people who are habitually late, clock them. You will find that they are usually late in the same amount of time each time, give or take a real emergency as opposed to the excuses they give. Once you know you have a forty-minute friend, you can adjust your time.

What Is Time and How Can I Have More of It?

In the '80s, the greatest compliment you could give people was to say they were busy. Did you carry an organizer book with you? Was a lot of your time spent calling to where you had been that day to track down your misplaced organizer? Relinquish busyness; experience more life. You only have time to live this moment, this moment.

How I Learned Pacing

I have a dear friend. He is in demand. His life is filled with interviews and performances and helping people and awards; through it all he is unflappable. I watched how he does it. He doesn't overwhelm himself with the pressure of the whole season or the whole week or even the whole day. He doesn't bottle it all up and worry about how to get through it all. He does one thing at a time. Imagine. One thing at a time. He's Mr. Cruise Control. No rushing and braking, just an even pace and it all gets done.

Know this: There's enough room for it all, and enough time for it all, and enough you for it all. Life is that big. If you want to give up anything, give up the notion that it has to be hard.

Here's an exercise to do (do it especially if you think you don't have time to do it). Close your eyes and experience a clock at your heart. What time is it—6:00 and you're half done; 3:10 and school's out? What do you associate with the time on your inner clock? Is it time to eat, time to play? Now ask your clock to show you how fast you run time. Let it show you if it goes round and round very fast or second by second. I just did it and it went very fast (which is exactly my travel schedule lately) and then all the numbers did a lilting dance and then laid down on the beach and basked in the sunshine, which is exactly what I did today. Gosh this works well.

What did your clock tell you about your inner rhythms? If you would like to expand time, work with the feeling that came up. If I'm rushing, I go to my inner clock and find that I'm the one who's pushing it. If you try to go faster than yourself, it takes longer. I can usually find what I'm doing in my body to contract time and then I adjust it. My breathing is constricted, so I breathe deeper; my neck is stiff, so

I let go of tension. When I relax those places of contraction, then the time on the clock expands.

How to Melt Your Clock

If you would like more time, play with your clock. Slow the second hand to slow motion. Have it be a Salvador Dali melted clock on the back of the chair and watch time drip into oblivion.

The shortest distance between the effort and result is to do just the effort that gets the direct result. Here's an instance of "impeccable" effort. I did this to get on an airplane.

The skycap said, "No you can't. It's too late. We can't take your luggage. It won't get on. You won't get on." What he was telling me was a four-hour layover in Cincinnati. No thank you. I was motivated; I went for the plane. I targeted gate 73. Meanwhile, I expanded time in myself and I concentrated; I used laser effort. I became the shortest distance between point A, where I was, and point B, where I needed to be in three minutes.

When you are pressed for time, always expand it, not contract it. Contraction gives you even less time. The way I expanded time was to slow down, to focus up, to tap a reservoir of calm within. Then I proceeded to walk steadily, and I concentrated. I did not, for instance, stop at the water fountain. My focus allowed me to walk at about ninety-two miles an hour while completely expanded on the inside. When you become the shortest distance between where you are and where you're going, no one gets in the way. You are laser effort. You set the beam. Nobody's going to mess with that beam.

I was dedicated to gate 73. When people saw me coming they stepped aside. When I got on the plane I switched from expanding time to contracting time, and it was a fast four-hour flight.

Now you may say, "What does time have to do with my being rich?" Abundance has a great deal to do with your feeling of enoughness around time. A sense of all the time in the world is true luxury.

Grief—The Secret to Joy

If you are a human being, and I assume you are, then what you are carrying around with you is grief. It's an integral part of what it means to be human. Earth is a tough place to live. It's hard to feel human feelings, and, as you know, it's harder not to feel them. I think that grief is the single most important activity for the '90s. We are finally releasing all our carried-around-feelings. Grief is going to reach critical mass. We're going to be letting out feelings in droves—together. Free of it.

Maybe that's why there's all this ecological talk lately about garbage. We are realizing that just because we stuff it in the dumpster doesn't mean it goes away. It's there; we need to find another use for it. Now we are having a new relationship with our inner garbage as well. Sort out your dumpster. Find value in what you stuffed away.

What Does Fear Look Like When You Face It?

It looks fine. It feels fine. The fear not felt is the one that hurts. The fear felt vaporizes and you are lightened —enlightened.

All our feelings all our life that we were afraid to feel are in us waiting to be felt. We want to let them out. We fear letting them out because we will feel loss, when the real loss is holding them in.

There are stages and phases of grief you go through: First, you don't want to accept that it's happened. You want to get the thing back, you want to get the person back or the marriage back or even if it's a sweater that you put in the washing machine and it comes out postage-stamp size. When John Lennon was shot, Yoko Ono said, "Say it isn't so." It's unacceptable. You can't wrap your head and heart around the fact that it's gone. At that point you will do anything that you can to have it not be so.

What's going on with loss is that if you have this huge clump of feared feelings, feelings like "I can't have that, I can't feel that empty, I can't be without my wife," then all of that, if it starts to come up, of course it's going to feel like loss because, guess what, it is! But it's not loss of that person. What it is loss of is the pain of keeping the feelings in.

The loss that you feel is really the loss of yourself, the loss of the familiar. The loss is "Oh gosh—who am I going to be? What am I going to do if I don't have this anymore?"

Who Am I Without You?

If you talk to people about their grief, notice their very real fear about who they are. I think a common thing that happens at funerals is that friends will say to the bereaved, "What are you going to do now?" And I think that's a human instinct that we're so smart about: the loss is ourselves, the loss is a shift in how we are going from living one way to looking at some issues around "Who am I and how do I go forward from here?" But it is a time to trust that the course is already set, that you have already determined these things—who you are, where you're going to go—for yourself, and that what is going on now is just your confidence in taking this step and the next step and the next one.

Reality Is a Figment of Your Imagination

This is a time to use the values you have within you about trust, and understanding that you're fine and that you are making it up as you go. That is the perfect way to do it. You don't have to have evolved plans that you're going to follow. The plan is there only to give your mind comfort.

Your mind creates an illusion of security that allows you to proceed, because where you're going to go is where you're going to go and has nothing whatever to do with where you *think* you're going.

One of the next stages of grief is when you accept that the person is dead. Also, this business about grief is that grief doesn't always happen when the person dies. There is something that happens when the person dies, but a great deal of grief work happens very many years later, triggered by loss of a job or a pet or other things entirely. It doesn't necessarily mean that the work within eighteen months after the death of a loved one isn't tremendous grief work then, but not everyone does that. Some of us put it in a pocket and wait. And that's perfectly legitimate, because we handle the thing when we can handle the thing, and that is the perfect time to handle the thing.

One of the next stages is that you will want to replace what was lost. For instance let's go back to the sweater that shrunk—your favorite sweater, of course, it's always your favorite sweater and then it comes out of the washer and it isn't itself anymore. You will have a tendency to try to get it back to its old self. You'll stretch and pull, which doesn't work. So then you'll say, "Okay it's gone and lost forever," and then you'll go out and you will hunt to re-create it. That causes pain. Not only do you not have your favorite sweater, but now any simulation of your favorite sweater falls vastly short. The new sweater that you get can't be itself; it has to be the old sweater. And if you'll remember the history of your old sweater, it took you maybe seven years to get it to feel that good. It wasn't your favorite sweater for maybe four years in the drawer. When you attach that responsibility to another sweater, to comfort you and be that for you, it's very painful because you feel not only the original loss, but you feel the frustration of much more profound loss.

You fear that not only have you lost your favorite sweater, but you fear you've lost the ten thousand things you associate with your sweater. (It was the sweater you play baseball in and now you fear that baseball is lost to you also.) Your grieving is multiplied by all the things you think you've lost along with the sweater. And you haven't lost those at all.

There's a fear there, and that's also why there's a fear of "who am I?" because it permeates you. It's "If I've lost (a) the sweater and (b) the ten thousand things I attached to the sweater, then one of the ten thousand things I attached to the sweater is me. I fear I lose me." You see the tremendous fear there is of loss of yourself.

That's why grief of a spouse has some amputation to it. The widow has to change her life entirely. Her entire life has gone into the casket with her dead husband, and a whole new life will begin for her. At first that is a loss of self; later it becomes a great opportunity for a gaining of a whole new self. But that's not how she feels initially.

When you are finally willing to say "That is lost to me," you relinquish having to re-create it, you relinquish the fear of losing all the things that are attached to it. And when you do that the spring buds of your new life shoot out of the soil. But you don't get to this stage until you are willing to relinquish, and surrender to the fact that what you had is gone.

Loss Is Always a Gain

When you relinquish there's another thing that happens that is so wonderful: once you let go and know that what you have lost is gone, it is—for the first time—there. Your dead loved one becomes a part of you. Example: Sometime after my mother died and I had grieved, I went traveling; my mother loved to travel. Wherever I went I saw her,

I saw items that she would have brought home. I was in Morocco and I saw great spangly-dangly earrings. They were mother earrings, no question about it. I bought them and wore them as a celebration of her. As I walked through the Casbah, there was a display of mirrors. And there in the thousand mirror images I saw my mother . . . in me. I realized that what I had done was internalize the best of her. There were parts that belonged to me that were from her. There I was in the thousand images.

So much of grief work is the shifting of how you feel about yourself and how you feel in terms of the relationship to your own dying. If you can let go of the fear that death is loss, you can experience that life has more gain.

Death, in fact, is where we most celebrate life. Grief wakes us to what it means to be alive. And what it means to be alive is underneath the cloud of feelings of loss, so that when we are so overwhelmed we can't possibly hold these feelings, then they have to come out. That is the use of tremendous loss: for us to understand that we can't carry that much sorrow and simultaneously have well-being, have an aliveness within us.

So it would behoove all of us to understand the value of grief and the reward—the deep gift we get at the bottom of it.

There is no such thing as loss. We don't usually believe that until we trust to let go.

The Difference Between Power and Control

Here's how to be powerful: Feel the feeling in your heart, *then* take the action with your head. The head and the heart do their jobs and not each other's. When you are willing and not afraid to feel the feelings, you are free. That freedom is the right use of power. If your head is doing your heart's job or your heart is doing your head's job, ever notice how dysfunctional you become?

Who's in Your Driver's Seat?

Who's in charge of you? Close your eyes and look. You can think of a control tower at your forehead; what does your control center look like? Mine is a bus. My heart drives my bus. Who's driving your bus? If the head drives, the heart has nothing to do but worry about where you're going. When the heart drives, that's intuition; then the head can be the navigator. The head can look at the map. It can do a really good job because it's doing jobs it's really good at doing. The heart can then drive. The head can see the map and say that the bridge is coming up two miles ahead; the heart knows the bridge is out. If the head is driving, the head and heart would have an argument. When the heart drives there's teamwork, there's expert discussion, each respecting each other's area of expertise. There's harmony between them, a good marriage of both, equally using all skills to their advantage rather than a power struggle of who's right.

Since my heart drives my bus, my relationship with myself has gotten much more loving. I don't fight me, and my relationship with others has gotten that harmony, too.

The Power of Power and Why We Don't Want It

Do you fear freedom? Here is a simple truth that we all know in the backs of our heads and are often too scared to acknowledge. If we have choices then we get to make them. Yet another revolutionary concept. The deal is, we don't want choices. They scare us. Choices require responsibility and we don't want to be responsible. We would rather say "I have no choice" than say "I have choices and make them." Power is when you are willing to see that you do have choice, that you can choose. Here is a simple lesson in the skill of making choices: Follow your heart's desire. Your heart knows where it is leading you. Have the strength of character to follow where it leads.

P.S. Not to worry about making choices about something you can't handle. None of this comes to you until you are ready. And the minute you are ready and ask, it comes instantaneously. I like a Zen saying: "All is in the readiness." Are you ready?

How Instant Is Instant Manifestation?

If we were living on the planet Zegazap, we'd think about a chair and it would appear and we'd sit down. We'd think the thought and the thing would be there. Why? Because as Zegazapians we could handle it when it got there. On earth, it can come instantaneously, too, but we usually walk right past it. With Feelization, once you think it then you realize that you already have it.

I Wanted It and I Got It

Understand clearer and clearer how you get exactly what it is you want. Put energy in feeling specifically how you want to feel when you get it. The clearer you can be about the specifics of what you want, the better the match. That doesn't mean you must make a list of all the details. It means that you can feel the essence of what you want it to feel like. The details will take care of themselves. It will be truer to what you want than what you are thinking in your head. For instance, if you want Mr. Right and Mr. Right has to be 6′2″ with brown eyes and thick hair, you might get exactly that, but meanwhile you forgot to mention that you wanted him to be nice to you. If you go to the essence of how you want to feel with Mr. Right, how you want to love him and how you want him to love you, how you want the feeling of being cherished, then you're free to have Mr. Right in the details that really matter. Lift off limited thinking that Mr. Right can only come in a 6′2″ package because 6′2″ does not mean love; it means tall. Once you release yourself from what it should look like, love is free to come to you in other forms such as a neighbor puppy who greets you loyally with face licks at your gate. Allow love to come in a much bigger package than 6′2″.

Life in Twenty-five Words or Less

You're smart. You've been living a life. What words of wisdom have you got to say to yourself? What can you impart as a result of the life lessons you've experienced?

Here's an example. I was on a road trip and happened upon a chic little bistro where I had a wonderful meal. When it was time to eat again I noticed I was holding out for another chic little bistro while I was hungry enough to eat the asphalt. Once I realized my rigid mindset, I pulled into the nearest IHOP and was free to have a deeply rhapsodic communion with pork links. I wrote this on the paper placemat:

The Answer to Life for a Tuesday, 1982

> A little of thising,
> and a little of thating,
> and knowing which, when.

What life lesson came to you on the interstate? What are your words of wisdom?

_____

_____

Here's a great example that was sent to me by Janice West Seaman about her Ozark pa, William West. When he was at an advanced age he was asked his life's philosophy.

> It's just plain common sense:
> Keep your head cool
> your heart warm
> your bowels open
> and your mouth shut.
> (any 3 of the 4 will get you through)

PART THREE

Being There

▪ *What It Feels Like When You Get There*

The way to get there is to be there.

The World Is Turning Right-Side Up

How the world appeared to work was in cause and effect. You do this, then this consequence occurs. You get a flat tire which makes you late for work, so you lose your job. How the world really works is, you want to lose your job so you get a flat tire. Do you see how clever you are? When we look at experiences in the old way it looks like we are victims of cirucmstances. That's no way to live. The other way, the new way, the better way, you can marvel at how powerful you are. You see your incredible ability to paint your own picture. It feels great. If you want to live in the old way, of "isn't it a shame," and "tsk" and "I'm too this or that," you'll always be the unhappy child of your dissatisfied heart.

Why History Will No Longer Be Able to Repeat Itself

As you know, a current problem is never about the current problem. The current problem is a way that we re-created an old situation so that we can solve it in a new way. Ask yourself, "Am I behaving toward this present situation using a past set of opinions?" Freedom is when you can respond to today's situation as today's situation and not a re-creation of an old pattern. When we are able to change our idea about our history (i.e., all men yell), then we clear up our future (i.e., ah, look, here's a softspoken man and another and another).

Downward Causation

Follow your heart. Go to essence. Let go of what it should look like outside yourself. Go directly to experiencing how it feels. This is real powerful stuff, and great fun. It takes us to the 21st century where we will be experiencing from our future backwards. We will no longer feel the need to climb out of our past to have a life now. Who we will be, determines who we are now.

We are at this time shifting from manifesting thoughts into physical reality. We are now going directly to manifesting feelings. We are now creating through feeling.

Use Feelization to feel your future in your heart and then have it in your life, today.

You have created your dream and your dream is coming true; it is not hard to achieve. What we humans have the hard time with is switching off channel 2, where we are presently living, and switching on channel 4, where our best possible future is going on now. It's up to us to join it already in progress.

The way to activate that switch is to use all your new tools. To move from surviving to thriving in your life. You can now put down the surviving tools and pick up the thriving tools. Here's a TIP: Trust, Intuition, and Patience are powerful thriving tools.

The more you are who you are, the more you'll get what you want.

To have what you want to have, be who you want to be; that helps you to do what you want to do, which allows you to have what you want to have.

What is natural happens naturally. What is yours comes to you. Your life is your own. Be of a receiving heart.

Being Abundant

If you want to be loved, love others.

If you want approval, approve of others.

If you want respect, respect others.

If you want to be heard, listen to others.

Then love yourself, approve of yourself, respect yourself, listen to yourself, and when you do, you will be loved, approved of, respected, heard.

If you want to be understood, understand. What you want, give it, and you will have it.

You can have anything you want, and you can have it with joy.

Love,

Dear One,

If you would like to write to me, I would love to hear from you. If you have written to me, thanks so much, I loved your last letter. However, you might be still waiting for a reply. As of this writing I'm about seven months behind on correspondence. So I have just now inaugurated a new policy. When I get your letter, I'll read it, and enjoy it, and enjoy you, and at that moment, I'll send you a sweet thought. That way you don't have to wait seven months to hear back. And I can then put the correspondence energy into writing my next book.

From my heart to yours,

Viki King
P.O. Box 563
Malibu, CA 90265